Islamic Economics and Finance

IE Business Publishing

IE Business Publishing and Palgrave Macmillan have launched a collection of high-quality books in the areas of Business and Management, Economics and Finance. This important series is characterized by innovative ideas and theories, entrepreneurial perspectives, academic rigor and practical approaches which will make these books invaluable to the business professional, scholar and student alike.

IE Business School is one of the world's leading institutions dedicated to educating business leaders. Palgrave Macmillan, part of Macmillan Group, has been serving the learning and professional sector for more than 160 years.

The series, put together by these eminent international partners, will enable executives, students, management scholars and professionals worldwide to have access to the most valuable information and critical new arguments and theories in the fields of Business and Management, Economics and Finance from the leading experts at IE Business School.

Islamic Economics and Finance

A European Perspective

Edited by

Jonathan Langton
IE Business School

Cristina Trullols
Director, SCIEF, IE Business School

and

Abdullah Q. Turkistani
Director of the Islamic Economics Research Center,
King Abdulaziz University

palgrave
macmillan

First published in 2011 by
PALGRAVE MACMILLAN

Palgrave Macmillan in the UK is an imprint of Macmillan Publishers Limited, registered in England, company number 785998, of Houndmills, Basingstoke, Hampshire RG21 6XS.

Palgrave Macmillan in the US is a division of St Martin's Press LLC, 175 Fifth Avenue, New York, NY 10010.

Palgrave Macmillan is the global academic imprint of the above companies and has companies and representatives throughout the world.

Palgrave® and Macmillan® are registered trademarks in the United States, the United Kingdom, Europe and other countries.

ISBN: 978–0–230–30027–9

This book is printed on paper suitable for recycling and made from fully managed and sustained forest sources. Logging, pulping and manufacturing processes are expected to conform to the environmental regulations of the country of origin.

A catalogue record for this book is available from the British Library.

A catalog record for this book is available from the Library of Congress.

10 9 8 7 6 5 4 3 2 1
20 19 18 17 16 15 14 13 12 11

Printed and bound in Great Britain by
CPI Antony Rowe, Chippenham and Eastbourne

Contents

Tables

Figures

Preface and Acknowledgements

This book is a result of the symposium 'Beyond the Crisis: Islamic Finance in the New Financial Order', hosted at IE Business School and organised by the Saudi–Spanish Center for Islamic Economics and Finance (formerly the Center for Islamic Economics and Finance, CIEF) and Casa Árabe International Institute of Arab and Muslim World Studies. It is an effort to take advantage of the excellent discussions that took place during the symposium, which form the major part of the book.

Part I is based on transcripts of audio recordings of the sessions. The transcript of the opening round table, where six distinguished speakers discussed contemporary issues in Islamic finance and the international financial crisis, is included in its entirety, with thanks to the speakers who participated. The transcripts of the workshops, which dealt with different aspects in Islamic finance, have been revised and summarised due to the number of participants involved and the desire to produce something more suitable for reading than the dynamic course of the dialogue that took place. In that process, every effort has been made to ensure that the comments of the delegates have been taken in their correct context and that their meaning has not been corrupted. Some parts have been rearranged in order to present similar ideas together. The reader should note that the treatment of a subject in the text may represent the contributions of several delegates, who may or may not have held the same opinion. If, as a result, the text at times appears inconsistent or self-contradictory, this reflects the reality of differing opinion around the subject.

Part II is a collection of chapters prepared as background information to complement the symposium or contributed afterwards by their authors as material relevant to this publication.

The editors would like to express their gratitude to certain people and institutions not mentioned elsewhere in this book. First to José Luis Pérez Estévez, former director of CIEF, and Elisa Meléndez Martín of the Center for Diversity in Global Management, IE Business School, who together organised and oversaw the symposium. Also to

King Abdulaziz University, which has been an important point of contact with the contributors from the Middle East, and to Casa Árabe for their support in Spain. Of course, it is important to acknowledge all those who have contributed their expertise and knowledge to the creation of this book, not just those specifically mentioned here, but also those who attended the symposium and shared their insights and experiences.

Finally, thanks must go to those institutions that sponsored the symposium, namely the Islamic Research and Training Institute of the Islamic Development Bank, The National Commercial Bank, Aljazira Bank, Al-Khabeer Capital, Madrid Centro Financiero and Invensys Rail Dimetronic.

Jonathan Langton, Cristina Trullols
and Abdullah Q. Turkistani

Foreword

In the early twenty-first century, financial knowledge has become the key element in our global community. The first decade began with the Enron and WorldCom scandals in 2002 and ended with the fall of Lehman Brothers in 2008, which caused the biggest financial crisis that global society has witnessed since 1929. By 2011, most people, regardless of their financial expertise, could name the major investment banks and explain their capitalisation problems and how the mortgage crisis developed. The second decade of the century has witnessed growing interest in new financial systems that could complement existing modes of finance, including ethical considerations that are not yet part of financial culture.

Today, the global economy dominates all aspects of social life. The financial markets, many of which are beyond the control of government, were the first to be globalised, leading to the free movement of capital. It seems that we are moving from a society dominated by political ideologies to a society dominated by financial interests. It is therefore no coincidence that various different intellectual groups have demanded reform of the international financial markets. As a result, popular demand for more ethical and human concern in the business sector has emerged, in both the West and the Islamic world.

In this regard, the financial markets have shown signs of convergence in Islamic and Western attitudes and behaviour, such as the sustainability movement. Indexes such as the Dow Jones Islamic Market Index (DJIMI) and the Dow Jones Sustainability Group Index (DJSGI) reflect a growing concern among investors to link financial results with ethical concerns. Although their history, subject matter, management and sources of funds might differ, the responsible investment movement and the Islamic investment movement are both responding to investors' desire to live their financial life according to their own values.

Sustainable industry, which aims to fulfil financial objectives while taking sustainability into consideration, is demand-driven, since people are increasingly educated about financial matters and want to ensure a more sustainable society. The majority of the sustainable financial movements that have emerged in recent decades, in both the Islamic world and Western markets, aim to give people freedom of choice in living their financial lives according to their own principles, and to foster more ethical corporate behaviour.

The Islamic economic system, which was first implemented on the international financial markets in the 1970s, has attracted attention in the aftermath of the financial crisis as an alternative mode of economy that can fulfil people's financial needs and meet their ethical requirements. Bankers estimate that the value of *Shari'a*-compliant assets rose to $895 billion in 2010 and that there are more than 450 *Shari'a*-compliant institutions and almost 200 traditional banks with *Shari'a* windows. Western financial institutions have become interested in understanding these phenomena and in finding ways to collaborate with the main players in the industry.

As Professor de la Torre (see Chapter 8) suggests, Islamic finance provides interesting formulas to prevent new crises, including the possibility of stabilising credit. It allows financing only when it is linked to value-creating real transactions, and therefore 'credit growth' is restricted by growth in productivity and income, creating a brake on uncontrollable credit growth in good years. In addition, systemic risk can be reduced if risk-management instruments are used in wealth-creating activities, as advised by Islamic financial practices. These practices meant that Islamic banks were far less affected by the derivatives meltdown that followed the demise of Lehman Brothers than were Western institutions. Islamic financial institutions are not freed from risk: restricting finance to physical assets can create asset bubbles as a result of an imbalance between liquidity and collateral, which could lead to a serious banking crisis. However, the fact that some of the tools used by the Islamic financial industry can add stability to the system is enough to warrant further study to see what complementarities might emerge from the two systems working together.

Working together is what lies behind this volume, the outcome of a collaboration that started in 2009 between the Islamic Economics Research Centre at King Abdulaziz University (KAU) and the Center for Diversity in Global Management at IE University. The collaboration sprang from the understanding that the Islamic financial market has developed as a serious alternative to (or partner for) conventional finance and that deeper knowledge of Islamic finance and of Islamic (and other sustainable) economic institutions, along with access to excellent research opportunities, will improve the ability of the next generation of financial experts to innovate and to find solid foundations on which to build the financial organisations of the future.

Both universities are interested in developing academic products that can empower future financial experts, and together they created the Saudi–Spanish Center for Islamic Economics and Finance (SCIEF) to leverage the experience of KAU and IE University in order to enhance awareness and knowledge of Islamic finance among Spanish and international businesses, state authorities and other interested parties. The efforts of the SCIEF and the two universities have culminated in this book, which provides insights into Islamic finance from some of the world's leading authorities in the field. The information in this book is relevant to both experts and non-experts in finance who want to know more about Islamic economics or grasp its fundamental principles.

This work has been made possible by the efforts of many people in Saudi Arabia, Spain and elsewhere in the world, among them students, executives, business people and international experts. Some of them have been acknowledged by name in the text, and some have not, and it would be impossible to mention them all; however, without their contributions, this book would not have reached publication. We would like to thank them all for their outstanding contributions.

The close collaboration between our two universities and two cultures has made us grow and learn something beyond the technical aspects of Islamic finance, helping us to understand each other and to be prepared for the difficult times that lie ahead in a world in turmoil. Working together towards common goals is the only way to move forward, acknowledging that human relations are still far more important than any technical solution.

Saudi–Spanish Center for
Islamic Economics and Finance

Contributors

Ibrahim Aboulola is a faculty member in the Economics Department, Faculty of Economics and Administration, King Abdulaziz University, Saudi Arabia. He has provided expert assistance to boards at the government level and in the private sector for rapid growth and prosperity. His areas of expertise include feasibility studies, privatisation techniques, financial training seminars, the evaluation and auditing of government reports and the supervision of Master's and PhD students.

Celia de Anca is Director of the Centre for Diversity in Global Management at IE Business School and a former Director of Corporate Programmes at the Euro-Arab Management School, Granada. De Anca has published regularly and is the co-author of *Managing Diversity in the Global Organization*. She is a member of the Ethics Committee of InverCaixa's Ethics Fund in Spain and a member of the Executive Committee at IE Business School.

Abderrazak Belabes is a researcher at the Islamic Economics Research Centre, King Abdulaziz University, Saudi Arabia. Belabes teaches the Geoeconomics of Islamic Finance module at the University of Strasbourg and the International Institute of Islamic Thought, Paris. His research interests include ethical finance, the regulatory framework of Islamic finance in Europe, curriculum development for Islamic finance and the dynamic of Islamic finance in France.

Ahmed Belouafi is a researcher at the Islamic Economics Research Centre, King Abdulaziz University, Saudi Arabia. Previously Belouafi worked for the Centre for Islamic Studies in Birmingham as an economics editor and a researcher. He was also a visiting lecturer at the University of Birmingham and a tutor at the London Open College. His research interests include curriculum development for Islamic finance, the development and spread of Islamic finance in Europe, financial crises and financial stability, and Islamic economics and finance literature by non-Muslims.

Alfredo Cabellos is a finance lawyer with Uría Menéndez in Madrid. He joined the firm in 2004 after working for several years in the finance departments of a number of Spanish and British law firms. Cabellos is primarily involved in asset finance, mainly in the shipping sector, using a variety of structures ranging from straight operating leases and loan facility agreements to leasings and tax-structured finance products. His work includes the drafting and implementation of security packages and insurance arrangements. In addition, he has extensive experience in transport and infrastructure project finance and in the negotiation and drafting of dry and wet aircraft leases. He is active with respect to regulations regarding public registries for assets.

Guillermo Canalejo is a tax partner with Uría Menéndez in Madrid. He has broad experience in corporate tax and has worked extensively in tax matters relating to cross-border investments and international tax planning, advising both foreign and Spanish-based multinationals. In addition, he is active in the development of tax-efficient financing, securitisation transactions and asset- and project-based financing, primarily in the transport and infrastructure industries. His practice is predominantly private equity transactions, collective investment vehicles and wealth tax planning. Canalejo co-chairs the Middle East practice group at Uría Menéndez. He is a regular contributor to a range of international tax publications and frequently speaks at conferences in Spain and abroad.

M. Umer Chapra is Research Advisor at the Islamic Research and Training Institute of the Islamic Development Bank. Prior to that, he worked for 35 years at the Saudi Arabian Monetary Agency, where he was actively involved in different phases of Saudi Arabia's hectic economic development. In appreciation for his services, he was awarded Saudi nationality by King Khalid in 1983. Chapra has taught at the Universities of Wisconsin and Kentucky and has worked in Pakistan at the Institute of Development Economics and the Islamic Research Institute. His seminal contributions to Islamic economics and finance span more than three decades, 15 books and monographs and more than 100 papers and book reviews. His most notable contributions are *Towards a Just Monetary System* (1985), *Islam and the Economic Challenge* (1992), *The Future of Economics: An Islamic Perspective* (2000) and *Muslim Civilization: The Causes of Decline and the Need for Reform* (2008). He has received a number of awards, including the Islamic Development Bank Award for Islamic Economics and the prestigious King Faysal International Award for Islamic Studies, both in 1990.

Guillermo de la Dehesa has served as the Spanish Secretary General of Industry and Energy, Secretary of State for Trade and Investment, and Secretary of State for Economy and Finance. He has been a member of the 113 Committee of the European Union and of ECOFIN, Deputy Governor of the IMF and the World Bank, and Governor of the Inter-American, Asian and African development banks. He has also worked at the Bank of Spain as Deputy Director General of International Relations. He is Honorary President of the Spanish Chambers of Commerce, and he is a member of the executive committee of the International Chamber of Commerce, based in Paris. In the field of economic research, he has been a trustee and member of the Group of Thirty (G30) in Washington since 1989 and a member of the Bretton Woods Committee since 1995, and he is Chairman of the Centre for Economic Policy Research, London. De la Dehesa is also Chairman of the Observatory of the European Central Bank, a Spanish European Central Bank watcher, and a member of the International Academy of Management and the American Economic Association.

Mohamed Ali Elgari is a former director of the Center for Research in Islamic Economics, King Abdulaziz University, Saudi Arabia. He is an expert at the Islamic Jurisprudence Academy of the OIC, the Islamic Jurisprudence Academy of the Islamic World League, and a member of the Shari'ah Council of the Accounting and Auditing Organization for Islamic Financial Institutions (AAOIFI). He is a member of the editorial board of several academic journals, including *Journal of the Jurisprudence Academy, Journal of Islamic Economic Studies* and *Journal of Islamic Economics*, and is on the advisory board of *Harvard Series in Islamic Law*. Elgari is a member of numerous *Shari'ah* boards of Islamic banks and *takaful* companies, among them the Dow Jones Islamic Market Index, the AAOIFI, the International Islamic Fund Market, Citi Islamic Investment Bank, HSBC Amanah, Merrill Lynch, NCB and SAMBA. He has published books and articles in Arabic and English and is a frequent speaker at conferences worldwide. In 2004, he received the Islamic Development Bank prize in Islamic Banking and Finance.

Fernando Fernández is a professor of Economics at IE Business School, where he is also Director of the Chair in International Financial Systems. He is an international consultant in macroeconomics and finance, Associate Director of DFC, President of Pividal

Consultores and an external advisor to the Strategy Committee at Arcano Financial Group. He was previously Chief Economist at Santander Central Hispano Bank and Senior Economist for the Western Hemisphere at the IMF. Fernández is a member of the editorial board of *El Economista* and a member of the Observatory of the European Central Bank. He contributes as a columnist to newspapers such as *ABC* and *El Economista* and as an economic and political analyst to several radio and television programmes. He also writes extensively in academic and regular journals and frequently speaks at national and international conferences.

Olivia Orozco de la Torre works at Casa Árabe and its International Institute of Arab and Muslim World Studies in Madrid, where she coordinates the Socioeconomics and Business programme. She has edited books on contemporary economic issues in Arab countries and is the chief editor of a bimonthly economics and business bulletin and webpage at Casa Árabe. She has co-authored the first book in Spanish about Islamic banking (with Alejandro Lorca, 1999) and has published articles on the subject and on the history of economic thought.

Ignacio de la Torre is Academic Director of the Master's in Finance programmes at IE Business School and a partner at Arcano Group. De la Torre has 14 years' experience in diverse fields of investment banking and spent 9 years as a professor on the Creative Accounting, Macroeconomics, Finance and Valuation courses at IE Business School. He has co-authored *El Final de la Crisis*, a book on the interrelations between finance and macroeconomics in the credit crisis, which was awarded the Everis Prize in 2009. His other publications include *Creative Accounting Exposed*, on creative accounting practices and detection mechanisms; *Los Templarios y el Origen de la Banca*, on the banking activities of Templar Knights during the thirteenth century; and *Islamismo: Desvelando el Radicalismo*, on the origins of Islamism. He has also published several academic articles on medieval history and on Islamic finance.

Note on Transliteration of Arabic Words

With respect to the use of Arabic words in the text, the transliterations in Part I have been italicised and, as far as possible, have been chosen to reflect the forms preferred by the Accounting and Auditing Organization for Islamic Financial Institutions (AAOIFI), a body that has prepared a number of widely accepted standards on Islamic finance. In Part II, the spellings of such terms are those of the individual authors.

Glossary of Selected Arabic Terms Related to Islamic Finance

fatwa	a religious ruling made by an Islamic scholar
fiqh	Islamic jurisprudence
gharar	uncertainty or risk
hadith	a pronouncement of the prophet Muhammad
halal	approved or lawful under Islamic law
haram	unacceptable or prohibited under Islamic law
ijarah	leasing
ijma'	consensus
ijtihad	interpretation
'inah	a spot sale followed by repurchase by the same party at a higher price on a deferred payment basis
istisna'a	a sale contract based on periodic advance payments for goods yet to be manufactured and to be delivered in the future
maqasid	the ultimate purpose, objectives and goals of Islamic law
maslaha	benefit or interest
maysir	gambling, or games of chance
mudaraba	a partnership in which one party provides capital to the other, who manages the investment; the profits being shared by both parties
mudarib	the manager or provider of labour and expertise in a mudaraba contract
murabaha	sale contract at an agreed mark-up or profit
musharaka	a joint venture, or partnership contract, both parties contributing capital to the investment, the profits and losses being shared by both parties
niyya	intention behind an act
qiyas	analogical reasoning
Qur'an	the sacred book of Islam
rab ul-mal	the investor or contributor of capital in mudaraba contracts
riba	usury or the charging of interest
sadaqah	voluntary charitable giving
salam	forward sale; full payment made for the future delivery of a good or service

Shari'a	Islamic law
sukuk	a financial certificate with certain similar characteristics to a conventional bond
takaful	a form of mutual guarantee used as a form of *Shari'a*-compliant insurance
wakalah	an agency contract under which the agent acts on behalf of the principal
waqf	endowment in perpetuity
zakah	obligatory annual contribution levied on Muslims of sufficient economic means

Part I

'Beyond the Crisis: Islamic Finance in the New Financial Order'

International Symposium on Islamic Economics and Finance

Organised by the Saudi–Spanish Center for Islamic Economics and Finance (formerly the Center for Islamic Economics and Finance), a collaboration between IE Business School and King Abdulaziz University and the Casa Árabe International Institute of Arabic and Muslim World Studies.

Hosted by IE Business School and Casa Árabe IEAM, Madrid, Spain, 16 and 17 June, 2010.

1
Opening Round Table

Madrid Stock Exchange (La Bolsa de Madrid), Madrid, Spain, 16 June 2010

The following is a transcript of the round table discussion held to open the symposium. It began with comments from the distinguished guests, each of whom spoke about their respective activities, the importance of Islamic economics and finance and the Saudi–Spanish Center for Islamic Economics and Finance at IE Business School.

Distinguished Guests

Antonio Zoido, President, Bolsas y Mercados Españoles
Rafael Puyol, Vice President, Institutional Relations, IE Business School
Gema Martín Muñoz, Director General, Casa Árabe
Ángel Martín Acebes, Vice President, ICEX
H.R.H. Prince Saud Bin Naif Bin Abdulaziz Al-Saud, Ambassador of the Kingdom of Saudi Arabia

Speakers

Guillermo de la Dehesa, Chairman of the International Advisory
   Board, IE Business School; Chairman, AVIVA; Vice Chairman,
   Goldman Sachs Europe; Member of the Board, Banco Santander
Celia de Anca, Director, Center for Diversity, IE Business School
Dr M. Umer Chapra, Advisor, Islamic Development Bank, Saudi
   Arabia
Dr Mohamed A. Elgari, former Director, Islamic Economics Research
   Center, KAU; Member of Shari'a Council, AAOIFI
Fernando Fernández, Professor of Economics, IE Business School
Ignacio de la Torre, Academic Director of Finance Programs, IE
   Business School; Partner, Arcano Group

> **de la Dehesa:** Good evening. My name is Guillermo de la Dehesa.
> I am the Chairman of the Advisory Board, IE Business School,
> and I am going to say a few words. I am not an expert in Islamic
> finance. Ask the two gentlemen who have come to speak about
> that. I have something in common with them – I have a beard.
> So that means I already have a necessary condition to be an
> expert in Islamic finance.
>
> **Elgari:** Necessary, but not sufficient! [*laughter*]
>
> **de la Dehesa:** In any case, I know a little bit about Islamic finance,
> and there is one area of Islamic finance that is very attractive to
> me – that is profit-sharing. I have been a big follower of
> Martin Weitzman, who has been one of the leading economists
> in the world writing about profit-sharing, or about loss-sharing,
> and I know that Islamic finance has worked pretty well through-
> out the crisis.
>
> I should be speaking about 'Beyond the Crisis' and 'the New
> Financial Order', and I could be very short. We are not beyond
> the crisis. And we haven't got a new financial order. So I could
> just stop here and leave. But, in any case, I am going to say a few
> things about both. The crisis is not over, as we know through a
> magnificent book written by two famous economists, Reinhart
> and Rogoff, called *This Time Is Different: Eight Centuries of
> Financial Folly*. They have put together 800 years of financial
> questions and studied them, because there are data from his-
> tory, and what they found out is that financial crises eventually

become debt crises. So we are now in a debt crisis. When banking credit goes up so much because of leverage and because of the demand, also, for credit, then banking debt and private debt, after a while, become public debt. So these are the two main issues that we should understand, because the government has to save the banks, and companies sometimes, and then take over the debt of the private sector, and it becomes a problem of public-sector debt as well. And we are in that situation.

So we are not beyond the crisis; we are still in this crisis. You see that the debt and deficits of European countries, and the United States also, have gone up very much and are becoming a problem, because now, in the case of Europe, markets have punished governments because, for instance, in Europe, the systems that were established to control the debt and the deficits of the governments have not functioned. The Stability and Growth Pact didn't work properly, so the markets eventually decided to discipline governments, and we are at this moment, in Europe, in that situation. Not in the case of the United States. Whenever there is a crisis, the bigger the crisis, the more money flows into the United States. So they don't care, because the spreads of the United States fall, instead of going up, because of its debts. So this is another interesting issue. But many of you have been investing in euros, and I know that many bankers and central banks have large stakes in euros, and I would say, 'Don't worry'. And I am going to explain why.

Don't worry.

First, because the core of the euro is Germany, France, Italy, I would say Spain, and the Netherlands. These five countries make up more than 82 per cent of the eurozone. And I don't think they are in any trouble. This is very important, because they are the core. The problem has arisen because a country that is only 2.2 per cent of the eurozone is in trouble. So the markets didn't react because it was only 2.2 per cent. But as the governments of the European Union didn't act in time, time passed, and no one was doing anything to help Greece, so eventually credit-rating agencies started to lower the ratings of Greece, spreads started to go up, and then, once spreads go up, rating agencies lower even more the rating, then spreads go up more, so eventually you inevitably go in to default. So this is why eventually the eurozone reacted strongly with this 'bazooka' of €750 billion that will be ready to help any government with problems.

So now the situation is the following. We already have a system to get help to any eurozone country that has problems, and as Europeans, we think that this is going to start going back to normal again soon, but it will take a little time because markets tend to react in this respect. One thing I would like to say. Some investors thought that the euro was going to break and the eurozone was going to break up. This is absolutely impossible. No country can get out of the euro – not Greece, not Germany – the two extremes; neither. If Greece decides to get out of the euro, then it has to change a law in the parliament. Let's say that changing this law takes only a week. In that week, all the citizens of Greece that have deposits in euros in the Greek banks, knowing that they are going to be converted into drachmas and that the drachma is going to fall fifty per cent against the euro, will go and get their deposits out and put them in euros in another country. That they can do today. All the banks and pension funds and investment funds that have debt in euros of Greece immediately will switch this debt; they will sell and buy other debts in euros. So before a decision is made by the parliament, the banks in the country will go broke. So this is something that cannot happen.

Let's look at the case of Germany. If Germany decides, for the same reason, that they want to get out of the euro, then the expectations of the Deutschmark increasing by fifty per cent, at least, against the euro will be terrifying, because Germany lives on exports. Internal demand has not been growing for ten years; this is why the growth is one per cent. They will not be able to survive if suddenly their exchange rate goes up fifty per cent. So there will be a rejection. People will start to riot in the streets to avoid that happening. So the euro is going to go on, the eurozone is going to go on, for the sake of the rest of the world, because the eurozone has a GDP close to that of the United States and is the largest importer in the world, above the United States. So if the eurozone goes bad, China will go bad, Saudi Arabia will have problems, everybody that is exporting to the largest importer in the world. So, let's have some common sense; going back would take some time. And then let's talk about important things like Islamic finance.

Thank you very much.

Unfortunately, I have to go. Otherwise I would add more fun to this evening.

de Anca: Thank you very much, Guillermo.

Ladies and gentlemen, welcome. We are very happy to be here with you, but I hope that in the future we can find ourselves in a better situation. I am surrounded by the most reputable economists in the world, so I would never try to even discuss any of the things they are discussing. My only role here will be [to] help them communicate with you all the things they have to say. But before we start this panel, I would very much like to thank our partners, King Abdulaziz University. It has been a very long year of hard work with all our friends, but I think it has been a very successful working initiative, and I'm sure this is the beginning of a very long, successful relationship. Thank you very much for being here.

As Guillermo was saying, there are two areas today. There is a new financial order, for which we have someone everyone from the Spanish audience knows, Fernando Fernández, one of the most reputable economists in Spain, and Ignacio de la Torre, economist and businessman, as well.

But before that, we also have to understand a little bit of what Islamic finance is, and for that reason we have Dr Umer Chapra. I keep on telling him that everybody who knows anything about Islamic economics has read his books, including myself; therefore everybody who knows anything about Islamic finance knows Dr Umer Chapra. And everybody also knows Dr Elgari, who is a very reputable economist and also sits on many international *Shari'a* boards, such as the Dow Jones, Citibank, UBS – you name it.

So, for that reason, what we are going to do now is, I will give the floor to the Islamic finance experts, to explain to us, for ten minutes each, a little bit about how they see the financial crisis from the Islamic financial perspective. Then I would like to call my two Spanish colleagues to open a dialogue on what we can do and how the new financial order will take shape. First I would like to give the floor to Dr Umer Chapra.

Chapra: Thanks a lot. It's a pleasure for me to be here to speak before this distinguished gathering, on a subject which has become very important after the current financial crisis. The world is looking for an alternative, and you may all be wanting to see whether Islamic finance is able to offer that alternative. If there is no solution to the current problem, the next crisis is going to be more serious that the present one. We don't know when the next crisis will come, but whenever it comes it will almost destroy the financial markets.

So, the first thing that we have to see, really, is what was the cause of this current financial crisis. The cause, which is generally accepted by most experts in the field, was excessive and imprudent lending. As a result of this, the debt around the world has increased considerably. It was only about $19 trillion in 2000. In 2010, it doubled to $38 trillion. It is expected to be $43 trillion in the year 2011, and we don't know how far it is going to go, because the prognosis is not very good. The US banks had free reserves only of about $50 billion at the time of the Lehman [Brothers] crisis. Now their reserves are about $800 billion. So you can see the reserves are 16 times more, and the extent of credit they would be able to create is going to be much higher, particularly because the rate of interest is at a very low level. So, this excessive and imprudent lending was one of the most important causes of the crisis.

Now the question is, why is this the case? The primary reason for this is lack of discipline in the current financial system. And what is it that creates this lack of discipline? The very simple answer is that, as a banker, you have reserves on the basis of which you can give credit, so you take collateral and give a loan, and the loan is usually about 60 per cent to 70 per cent of the collateral. So when the collateral is available, the banks are willing to give the loan. It is a very rare situation where the value of collateral falls as rapidly as it fell in the United States. So, they were able to give a lot of credit, and this situation goes on.

Now, there arose some innovation in the financial markets which changed the situation dramatically in favour of debt expansion. This was securitisation, or sale of debt. Securitisation enabled banks to give more and more credit. Of course, previously it was not possible for them to sell sub-prime debt. What securitisation did was enable them to sell even sub-prime debt, when the two were mixed together and securities were sold and people did not really know what was the extent of sub-prime debt in this security. So, the debt expanded very rapidly; then Collateralised Debt Obligations protected them even more, because they could give debt and then protect themselves by buying insurance. Credit Default Swaps were a form of insurance. Then there was the failure of the ratings agencies, because the ratings agencies had a vested interest in the banks themselves, and they were willing to give a better rating to the debt scrips of these banks. Then there was the concept of 'too big to fail'.

The supervisors also failed because Mr Greenspan was in favour of liberalism, and he went too far in this case. There is no doubt that there is a need for some liberalism, but the job of the central banks is to ensure that things do not go too far. There was a great deal of cheating going on, and Mr Bernanke himself says that abusive, unfair and deceptive lending practices were being used. If these deceptive practices were being used, what was the central bank doing? Isn't one of their major jobs to ensure that such practices do not take place? And if they are taking place, they need to be curbed. Even Christopher Cox, Chairman of the Securities and Exchange Commission, says that many laws were being broken, and if laws are being broken, and the Chairman of the Securities and Exchange Commission sits and talks about liberalism, well of course the crisis is bound to come.

So, now, in what way can Islamic finance really help? First of all, it has to inject a moral dimension into the financial system. See, the notional amount of outstanding derivatives had risen to $692 trillion, and a substantial part of this was not genuine derivatives. They were what are called 'naked derivatives', 'naked swaps', in other words, [...] if I have given a loan and I buy insurance in the form of a debt swap, well it is alright, but if I have not given a loan to anybody, and I still buy swaps – and many people do that – then naturally the market is going to be overloaded with risk. Six hundred and ninety-two trillion dollars of outstanding derivatives were there in March 2009, and the world GDP was only $57 trillion. So, these derivatives took 12 times the world's GDP, and since most of these were naked derivatives, the market was ultimately not going to be able to bear this risk, and there was a failure.

So, in what way can Islamic finance help? Can it help reduce the extent of debt in the market? Yes, because in the Islamic financial system there is no lending and borrowing as such. I cannot lend money to you and I cannot borrow money from you. The debt takes place as a result of the sale of goods or services. I sell goods to you on the basis of credit. I cannot lend money to you because I am not allowed to charge interest, and if I am not allowed to charge interest, why would I give money to someone like this, except when it is charitable financing for some person who is in difficulty; I may give an interest-free loan to him. But otherwise, in the market itself, there is not going to be any lending and borrowing except through sale and purchase of goods and services. So, this is a very important aspect of Islamic finance, because this links the debt to the real sector of the economy. In other words, debt cannot expand more than the growth of the economy. And if the debt expansion is curtailed in this manner, then naturally we have a very strong factor which is going to reduce the possibility of such a crisis occurring.

What are the suggestions to the international financial system on the basis of Islamic finance? What kind of a reform is needed? First of all, the most important reform that needs to be brought about is to raise the share of equity and lower that of debt in total financing. Debt has gone too far, as I have already indicated by means of figures, and there are a number of scholars, even in the Western world, who feel that the ratio of equity needs to be raised.

[*break in recording*]

...Professor Kenneth Rogoff of Harvard. He says, 'In an ideal world, equity and direct investment would play a much bigger role.' So, the role of equity and direct investment needs to be increased, and that means that leverage needs to be controlled. Leverage has been very high in some areas of the Western financial system. When the long-term financial capital failed, at that particular time its leverage was 67:1; in other words it had borrowed $67 for only $1 of its capital. Any institution which has such a high amount of debt will not be able to repay any, and, if it gets into difficulty, it is going to create problems for the financial system. So, the fact that the debt has been increasing very rapidly is one of the major factors, and it needs to be controlled by increasing the share of equity and lowering the share of debt in total financing. The other thing is to allow credit primarily for promoting development of the real sector. As in the Islamic financial system, if credit is linked to the real sector, then, of course, there cannot be excessive expansion of credit.

Requiring banks to hold debt until maturity. This was a system prevailing, even in the West, for a long time. It is only in recent decades that it has been forsaken. When a bank is able to give debt and then sell it, it does not have any incentive to underwrite the debt carefully, because you are going to pass the risk anyway. And if the banks give the debt, then sell it, they have passed the risk and reduced their own risk, which means they can go on lending. Within the Islamic financial system, it is not possible to sell debt. Why this restriction? Because, if this is done, then the banks will have an incentive to underwrite the debt carefully, and they will not go on lending more and more without crucial examination of the debt proposal. CDSs, even if they are created in the Western world – and there is no harm in this – but they should not be allowed to become instruments for wagering. There should not be 'naked' CDSs, only those CDSs which are meant to insure the actual debt given, and not naked debts.

And all financial institutions need to be regulated. This is, of course, against some of the principles Mr Greenspan sued for. He was for liberalism, total liberalism, and a lot of this chaos was going on in the financial system, and he was not willing to take any action, because he thought that the market itself would be able to take care of this problem. But the market was not able to take care of it, and the central bank also did not intervene, so things went on getting worse and worse. So, all financial institutions need to be regulated; not only commercial banks, but all institutions that operate in the financial market.

These are some of the reforms that need to be undertaken in the financial system to save it from future crises. But, if the reform is not undertaken, then we should be aware of another crisis which is going to be more serious than the present one. And as I indicated to you, at the time of the Lehman [Brothers] failure, the total reserves of US commercial banks were only $50 billion. Now they are already about $800 billion, sixteen times more. Their ability to lend more has increased substantially, and the rate of interest is low, so you can imagine what is going to happen. So, if the reforms are not undertaken, the next crisis will be even more serious than the present one. Let us hope that this does not take place.

Thank you.

de Anca: I would like now to give the floor to Dr Elgari to also explain his vision from the Islamic point of view about the crisis.

Elgari: I am honoured to be with you today to present views which are shared by my fellow Islamic bankers and Islamic economists, on the current financial crisis.

Islamic finance has advanced a lot, from a simple idea, over thirty years ago, to become an industry that exceeds $3 billion globally. Islamic finance brings solutions aligned with Islamic observance, which, according to the established rules of *Shari'a*, equate interest-based lending to usury, which, again, is repugnant to the Qur'anic teachings, which prohibit making money out of money. Islamic banking is not a form of worship, so it's good for everybody. But Islamic banking is a manifestation of human values, of equity, justice and fair play in markets. The main purpose of my speech today is simply to start a conversation. To communicate to this most august gathering another side of the story, in the hope that we may contribute, albeit very modestly, to the debate that is taking place today, which will eventually shape the world financial system for decades to come.

If we examine, probe and analyse all the *Shari'a* injunctions in the realm of finance, we see a clear thread, a common denominator, leading to an unmistakable conclusion: that the basic sector in the economy is one which produces real goods and services. Money is only a lubricant. Money is a facilitator. It is not, by itself, a commercial enterprise. This may sound simple, maybe simplistic, but making sure that money remains a medium of exchange and a store of value, and not itself a producer of value, is the essence of any serious reform of the financial system. The overall impact of such a rule can easily be seen by any student of economics. The challenge was, and is, how to transform such a basic principle into policy and into rules of behaviour and a system of ethics that eventually creates a self-regulating system that guarantees both stability of the economy and equitable distribution of income and wealth.

Ladies and gentlemen, I claim that Islamic law has all it takes to achieve this. It starts with the prohibition of *riba*, or usury, which is defined in a specfic way as the stipulated increase in loans, i.e. interest. There is no justification for money itself creating an added value by the mere passing of time; in other words, money made out of money.

Making money out of the exchange of goods and services is permitted; it is not prohibited from the *Shari'a* point of view, even if it is only temporal. Money here is only a medium of exchange. Value is created by the other side of the transaction where labour and capital are mixed to produce goods and services. Furthermore, once the debt obligation is fixed, it cannot increase, for any reason. Any increase is also, from a *Shari'a* point of view, usurious. Why? Because, permitting such increase effectively means creating value from pure monetary transactions, involving more tomorrow for less today for the same subject matter. We are not at all denying the time value of money; we are only recognising it when money is exchanged for goods and services, not money for money.

The circle will not be complete unless we further prohibit the discounting of loans, since such action boils down to, again, creating value out of money itself. This is why *Shari'a* also prohibits such acts, which are referred to in the jurisprudence of *Shari'a* as 'sale of debt'. Furthermore, it would be simplistic to think that money is just the local currency. It would have been very easy to circumvent all the above prohibitions by simply exchanging one currency for another, to be delivered in the future, thus pretending that the value is created from exchange of money for something else. Money, from a *Shari'a* point of view, is what people use as a medium of exchange. Whenever this thing is traded for another medium of exchange, it can only be done on a spot basis. Forces of supply and demand can determine the rate of exchange, but only reflecting the value of the currency itself, not the value of the passing of time.

I can go on and on.

Suffice it to say that, if all these injunctions are followed, there is no way an economy would face a crisis like the one we are facing today. This is the fact of the matter. This is the crux of the problem and the kernel of the solution. In an interview a few months ago, Nobel laureate economist Professor Amartya Sen, in answering the question 'What exactly has gone wrong with our financial system?', said 'It is too much money-for-money transactions.' How true, but we knew this 1400 years ago, because everything I just narrated to you is mentioned in our scriptures, the *Qur'an,* and the sayings of the prophet Muhammad. It is also astounding and extraordinary the length, the depth, the detail, to which the Islamic economic system, which derives its rule from *Shari'a*, has gone to seal the door to every transaction that steers the financial sector away from being just a facilitator, from being a smoother, to being complete in itself – appropriating value that is created in the real sector.

An example: The now fashionable non-recourse mortgage, which contributed, not in a small way, to bringing havoc to the mortgage market in the United States, is prohibited, by name, in *Shari'a*! This prohibition was narrated in an authentic dictum by the prophet Muhammad himself. We know that a standard mortgage is permitted; it is even mentioned in the *Qur'an.* But the non-recourse mortgage shifts all the risks to one party, thus violating one of the established rules of *Shari'a* related to fair play in the markets.

Ladies and gentlemen, my message to you today is very simple. We are the ancestors [*sic*] of a great civilisation. Some of its achievements stand very tall and were preserved for the world to see by the people of this great country. We have so much to contribute to the human effort, to rid the world of the cancer that has ruined the financial system worldwide. This cancer is the relentless attempt of financial pundits to make money out of money. Otherwise, how can we comprehend that for each dollar representing a real trade transaction, there are one thousand dollars of money-for-money transactions? When the GDP of the whole world was only $66 trillion in 2007, the derivatives market in the United States alone was in excess of $516 trillion. There is a language we all speak. There is a right and wrong we can all recognise. It is wrong to make money out of money. All we need now is to translate this simple wisdom into policy.

Thank you very much, ladies and gentlemen.

de Anca: Thank you very much, Dr Elgari.

Now, Dr Fernández, I would like to ask you, from a Western point of view, about reforms. Dr Chapra and Dr Elgari have been talking about the crisis and the potential reforms. Do you see that differently? The things they say, like equity and direct investment linking the real economy, from a Western point of view, is that different, the reform of the new financial order? Your views on that?

Fernández: Thank you very much, Celia. It's a pleasure to be here and share this audience with these distinguished scholars. I am at a clear disadvantage here because, first of all, I am not an expert in Islamic finance, like Guillermo. I don't even have a beard! So, I can't even join him in that respect. I don't even have hair, so that makes it even more difficult!

[*laughter*]

Having said that, I will try to make some sense in my remarks. I personally believe that we are way past the blame game in interpreting the financial crisis. It is there – we have to deal with it. We can write all sorts of books about what went wrong. We know for sure that one thing went wrong – credit growth was excessive. If there is any common trend in financial crises in these '800 Years of Financial Folly' that Guillermo was referring to in that book by Carmen Reinhart and Kenneth Rogoff, it is that whenever credit growth is excessive, we have a problem.

It may take two years, it may take five years to show, but we will have a problem. And the problem is called imprudent lending – as somebody said, bad loans and a debt crisis. This is where we are and what we have to deal with.

Unfortunately, I will try to stay away from making any ethical or value judgements on moral issues; I am in no way an expert. I feel personally rather uncomfortable in those discussions. I have no way to address them, so I will have to restrict my comments to the way we see finance and the way we conduct finance. I am not assuming, or pretending, that this is good or bad, wrong or right, just that this is the way we do it and the way we will keep doing it.

Let me play, a little bit, the devil's advocate, if I may use that moral expression. Crises are human in nature, and crises respond, basically, to economic cycles and psychological cycles. If we take the route of basing credit only on physical assets, which is something that I have understood defines, to some extent, Islamic finance, we do not solve the problem of the valuation of those physical assets. We still have the problem of how to value those assets. Just by linking credit, loans, to whatever physical asset we can think of – land is a perfect example in terms of mortgages – we do not avoid the problem of excessive lending. We still have the problem of the valuation of those physical assets. Unfortunately, valuation responds to supply and demand, and therefore valuation responds to 'animal spirits', to use an expression we are familiar with. Those animal spirits run very wild at some points, and they were wild for a while. So we have a problem with the underlying valuation of those physical assets, which I think has very little to do with the system of finance that we organised.

It is also my point – how shall I say this? – my assumption, I guess, because it is not based on any thorough research. This is my assumption: that Islamic banks were saved from the financial crisis, not because of the system of Islamic finance, but because of the fact that they had a lot of savings, because they were relying on a huge pool of savings. Whereas Spanish banks – Western banks, if you want to use that expression – were based on very little savings because the population of those countries save very little, so we had to take the money from somewhere else. So, I think that has a lot more to do with reserves and the point that was raised by Dr Chapra when he mentioned that the equity–debt ratio was probably wrong, and we do have to review this concept. In fact, early discussion on the financial-sector reform, the famous Basel III, whatever that is – it is something we all talk about; no one has read it because it hasn't been written yet – but what we know is that one of the underlying conclusions in that document, if you read the material produced by the Financial Stability Board of the BIS, the Bank for International Settlements, will have to do with increased capital for banks. We know that for sure. That will come. Which addresses, I think, the point of having, or not having, enough reserves.

Now, there was another point that was raised by Professor Chapra, which I found very interesting, and this is requiring banks to hold debt to maturity. If we were to do that, and I am not even going into a discussion of if this is good or bad, desirable or undesirable, but what I do know is that if we were to do that, consumers, mortgage owners and governments in the Western world will have a serious problem. The secondary market will disappear, essentially. There is no reason to have secondary markets if debts are held to maturity. So, a large part of the way we finance, the way we are used to dealing with private, business and government finance, will have to change. And this is my second point. We have a tendency, as we've seen in previous crises, to over-react. Not only are markets wild and over-shoot [*sic*], but governments and regulation also over-shoot. We have to strike a balance, sort of a cost–benefit analysis, between making sure that we have no crisis in the future and making sure that we have some economic growth and some economic activity in the future. Because, whether we like it or not, the last twenty-five years, overall, have been the most successful years in the economic history of the world. And the jury is still out. Even if we take a five per cent drop in GDP in most industrialised countries for the next five years, which is not a minimal crisis, and we take a long average, still the Western world would have grown, in the last twenty-five years, including those five crisis years, at a greater rate than at any other previous point in history. So we may take a long perspective in time, and we may see things differently.

Now, having said this, I was challenged by Professor Elgari's comments on making money out of money and basing every-thing on real goods and services. It reminded me a little bit of – those of us in the Western tradition probably remember – the discussion that the Physiocrats had way back in the eighteenth century in France. I was so challenged by those remarks that I was tempted to answer them, but I will refrain, because this is a discussion we have had for so many years, and my personal conclusion is that it is so hard to distinguish when you are mak-ing money out of money or making money out of a physical asset which underlies money. Let's take land. How do you make money out of land? What is the difference between holding land and holding money? From a purely accounting point of view, what is the difference between storing value in land or in money? Is there really a difference? I don't know. I'm sure there is an ethical difference, a moral difference, I'm not talking about that, I have no idea about that. But from a purely radical eco-nomic point of view, I'm not sure there is a difference.

The final point I want to make, which I think is probably the most interesting to this audience, is that Islamic finance really doesn't need to be envisaged as a radical alternative to, let's call it, Western finance, or Occidental, or whatever other qualifica-tion you want to make, to be of significance to Western research-ers and financiers. We may be a very pragmatic society, but the way I like to look at these things is that there is an alternative pool of resources out there. They have the rules. They have the right to have those rules. Can we play by those rules? Is it useful to us to understand those rules, respect those rules and benefit from those rules: in terms of our business, our companies, our banks, our governments and, in the end, the population? It is therefore, to me, not so much a discussion of whether the two systems are alternatives, or even a sort of competition: who is superior to whom, which financial system will win? That, to me, is really not the point. The point is, can we work together? Can we benefit together from different rules, and there seems to me an obvious answer to that point, and probably that is what Celia de Anca wanted me to say, but I do believe it. We have a problem – Guillermo said it. In Spain, in Europe and in the US, we have a lot of debt. We have a large pool of debt, and it will be with us for many years. And there is a large pool of savings in the Gulf countries, because they have been more prudent, or more successful, or more lucky; it doesn't matter to me. The fact is that they have a very large pool of savings and a very large pool of resources, which we need. So, can we make it attractive? Can we make a win–win situation, a win–win deal? Maybe I am taking a too pragmatic, purely rational, Western investment bank attitude to the problem, but this is the way I was raised, I was brought up. This is the way I have framed my mind, and I am too old to change it now. But I do think it is to the benefit of all of us if we design a way by which we both can benefit. Are we able to introduce financial products that meet Islamic requirements, and are we willing to tap those resources? I think the obvious answer, from the Spanish point of view, is that we should be able to do this, because we need those resources, and I find no objection in any way to respecting everybody's values. This is for them to decide. It is for us to decide if we are going to change our legislation to allow this to become an additional source of funding, an additional source of finance. Is it so difficult to do it? Can't we learn from other countries that have done it? It didn't seem to be so difficult in other European countries. Can we do this? Should we do this? The answer is clearly 'yes' to me.

I hope I haven't been too provocative or too radically practical, but as I said, this is the way I am used to thinking. Thank you.

de Anca: Thank you, Fernando. You've been raising some provocative thoughts, as usual, but that's probably why you are here. Before allowing our friends on the floor to react, I would first like to ask Ignacio as well. Fernando's last point being a little pragmatic, we can go back to the theory for a little while before closing if you wish. Can we play with those rules? You know both; you know how Islamic finance works in a very practical way, and you know Spanish industry. Do you think we can play with those rules?

de la Torre: Thank you and welcome to our Saudi friends.

I met a person once who was seventy and he told me 'I would never send my son to a business school.' I said, 'Why?'

He said, 'Because the first thing you teach him is how much debt to put on the balance sheet, and, actually, my company never had any debt in the last 100 years'.

And this is basically the topic of the discussion we are having today. I teach accounting, and what we say about the balance sheet of Western banks is that on the left side there is nothing right, and on the right side there is nothing left!

[*laughter*]

And this is linked to the level of debt and leverage which is in the system. If you look at JP Morgan in the year 1900, the level of equity to total assets was one-third, and today the relationship is 1 unit of equity against 24 or 25 of debt, and this is the main problem we are facing. Now, I agree that the solution is moving back towards a level with a higher level of equity – the problem is that if we do it now, there wouldn't be any money to lend to people or to companies, and we would go into another crisis. So we need to do it, but not to do it now. This is the main problem.

I also agree with Fernando that, in the end, people just answer to different human incentives, and people were incentivised to borrow due to the fact that interest rates were very low. That could be the fault of Mr Greenspan, or it could be the fault of the Chinese who were putting their money in US bonds, so the interest rates went down, and so everyone was easily obtaining credit. I think a part of the problem here was with politicians. People don't remember that US banks were forced to lend to sub-prime: they were forced to lend by Jimmy Carter, and they were forced to lend by Bill Clinton. They made rules that forced US banks to enter into sub-prime, and people forget that the major bankruptcy here was not that of Lehman Brothers, it was of the government-sponsored entities, 'Freddie Mac' and 'Fannie Mae' – $5 trillion – and both were government-sponsored entities with a lot of regulation. So, in the end, I think it is a question of incentives. So, answering your question, I think that we have some important lessons to learn from Islamic finance, and they are linked to financial stability.

First, I agree you need to put some brakes on the ability of the banker to expand the balance sheet; because, in the end, the banker is going to answer the incentives. If your remuneration depends on the share price and the share price depends on the return on equity, then you have an incentive to put as much debt as possible in the balance sheet, to reduce the level of equity so you increase the return on equity. So you need to put some brakes on, to keep the bankers from expanding the balance sheet at 20 per cent per annum. And I think it is true that linking some of the credit growth to physical assets could be one of these brakes. The problem, and I think you have a point Fernando, is that if Islamic finance grows and grows and grows, and all of this liquidity is poured into physical assets, you can create a bubble in the valuation of these physical assets, such as housing. There is a new mortgage law in Saudi Arabia, and if a lot of Islamic money is channelled into financing these mortgages, then you could have a real estate bubble due to this problem of demand and offering.

Also, I do agree that there should be some limit to the level of debt-to-equity you consider when investing. In Islamic finance, you cannot put money into a company which has a debt-to-equity above one-third. I think this is a very healthy rule when selecting some companies. I think that the incentives we have in the West clearly favour the use of debt, which is cheaper because of the taxman and because of politicians as well. So, probably we should think about changing the tax rules, or perhaps not discriminating equity against debt is something to consider.

In terms of derivatives, Islamic finance, in general, allows for derivatives as a tool to hedge, not as a tool to bet. The only thing is that, even though I think it makes a lot of sense for banks just to use derivatives to hedge, [they should not be used in] proprietary trading, because in the end it is ourselves, citizens, rescuing banks if the bet does not go well.

I think that there is a little bit of confusion with the statistics of derivatives. It is right that derivatives are ten, eleven, twelve times the size of GDP, but if I bet $1 against $10 million that the interest rate will go up, the notional amount of money is $10 million, but I am just betting $1. The real money behind these bets of derivatives is just $20 trillion, not $700 trillion, and this is basically the money that is actually at risk, which is much lower.

I also agree that there is a key point in Islamic finance in that you have huge control on the first loss. The main problem behind this crisis was that I was giving money to a person who couldn't repay it, and I was selling this credit to a third person, so I just wouldn't care to whom I gave the money. This is changing now in US regulations. Now it is forbidden to sell 100 per cent of a credit, and you must retain the first 3 per cent, and you cannot hedge this 3 per cent, to make sure that you will never give money to someone who cannot afford it. In Spain, we already have this situation, because when we sell a mortgage, normally the investors, who tend to be the Germans, want to make sure that, if there is a non-performing loan, the Spanish bank loses the first 3 per cent. This is a practical thing which I think has helped some of the mortgage investments in Spain be of a much better quality than the US ones.

Also for the audience, I think there is a key point here on the relevance of what we are dealing with today. We are talking of an industry which is $1 trillion, it's one per cent of global savings, and it's growing at 20 per cent per annum, so there is plenty of liquidity in this system, in the Islamic banking system. I have been to Saudi Arabia twice. I have spoken to Islamic bankers, and there is plenty, plenty of liquidity. And I think that's why we should be putting all of our efforts into exploiting this opportunity. Also, take into account that every Western government is just looking for finance in the sovereign wealth funds, which are not Islamic finance-oriented, and I think we should be doing our homework to exploit this opportunity, which is much better and much less competitive. And the relevance is basically Saudi Arabia. Saudi Arabia is going to be the the key country in the GCC. There will be a monetary union, and the central bank will be based in Riyadh. So, within that, the main actor in the region and in the Islamic finance industry in the future will be Saudi Arabia.

Finally, let me just address the opportunity. London has already worked to transform the regime in the UK to attract

Islamic finance. Paris has been doing some work in the last year. There has been a German autonomous government, Saxony-Anhalt, who issued a *sukuk*, which is a type of instrument traded through Islamic finance, in 2003. Also, Singapore has issued a *sukuk*. In Spain, we are good at energy, renewable energy and infrastructure, which are great assets to be used as collateral for Islamic finance. So, I think there is a lot of work to be done for Spanish politicians, who have not done anything up to now, in order to look for this opportunity. Let me just tell you that General Electric, which is one of the most important companies in the world, just issued a *sukuk* of $500 million, which proves to you that this is a reality and that many Western companies can obtain finance through Islamic finance.

Many thanks.

de Anca: Thank you very much, Doctor.

I think we have about 15 minutes where I would like us to have a discussion. Of course, many of these issues, as Fernando was saying, have been around since the Physiocrats and, I would think, probably since Ibn Khaldun have been in the open. So, I don't think that in 15 minutes we can get any real conclusion. However, I think, [Dr Elgari, since some of the provocative thoughts were in response to your words], you have the right to react to some of the thoughts of Fernando if you would like to take the floor to say something.

Elgari: My colleague, the beardless Fernando, said that he does not want to engage in the ethical. Well, leave this to me.

[*laughter*]

Ethics is the most important aspect of any social organisation, because if people lose their guidance, as far as the ethical aspect of what they do, then they are going into a crisis of sorts. Now, one of the unique things about Islamic banks is that every Islamic bank has a *Shari'a* board. The *Shari'a* board is membered [*sic*] by people who are from outside the institution, who are keen to make sure that the institution never forgets that it belongs to a society which has values cherished by every individual and that have to be adhered to. This is very important because you need, sometimes, a reminder that ethics is important. And the second point I'd like to address here is, again, my neighbour here said that it is an established fact that Islamic banks were more or less saved from the effects of the crisis, and maybe the reason is because they have too much liquidity. The fact of the matter is that none of them engaged in the 'now you see it, now you don't', these CDOs, CDSs and the rest of them, especially the ones that are pure wagering. There is no economic sense, except that people like to gamble, as with the CDS. Even a few weeks before the collapse of Lehman Brothers, Lehman Brothers itself was trying to push these things into Islamic banks, and *Shari'a* boards have steadfastly refused to accept any justification for investing in things. And that's the reason we're saved. Thank you.

de Anca: Before Fernando, I would like to give the floor to Dr Chapra, who also wanted to react.

Chapra: Thank you very much. Dr Fernando said that Islamic finance is not a radical alternative. This is, of course, true. A number of the principles of Islamic finance have been a part of the Western tradition. It is only in recent decades that those principles have been forsaken and brought difficulties to the financial system, because after all many of these principles that Islamic finance has have also been taught by other religions. As the *Qur'an* clearly says, 'Nothing is being said to you what was not said to the prophets before you', and these principles are universal because these messengers of God came to every society. So, it is not really a radical alternative. These principles are, or have been, a part of Western tradition, and what Islamic finance is trying to do is bring back some of these into the financial system in the world once again. So, this is certainly true; this is not a radical alternative, and we can benefit from each other. Islamic finance can learn a lot from conventional finance, and conventional finance can learn a great deal from Islamic finance. And if some of the principles of Islamic finance are taken by Western finance, I think it will be very useful for the stability of the financial system around the world. Thank you.

de Anca: Thank you very much, Dr Chapra. I think we will have time for one or two questions from the floor, because I see you've been patient. One or two, but probably no more.

Bashir Khouri: My name is Bashir Khouri. I am a Lebanese journalist. I have this simple question to ask. If the main cause of the crisis was excessive lending, why is the solution adopting the principles of Islamic finance and not controlling lending activities instead? And I am going to share with you the experience of the Lebanese banking sector, which is being studied everywhere in the world, because apparently it's a case study. Lebanese banks, most of which are traditional, non-Islamic banks, were also able to overcome the crisis. You most probably know that Lebanon is a country where people know very well about *Shari'a,* since half of the population, or even more, is Muslim. But Lebanese banks, traditional banks, were able to overcome the crisis simply because the central bank in Lebanon worked very, very hard to prohibit commercial banks investing in what we call 'toxic' financial products. And despite the high level of liquidity we have right now – especially after the international crisis, because many remittances were sent to Lebanon after the crisis and now we benefit from a high level of liquidity – despite all this the total credits in the Lebanese market represent around two-thirds of the GDP, because the central bank is being very strict on this level and doesn't want the lending activity to grow in such a way that it leads to what happened on the international level. I just wanted to share this experience, the Lebanese experience. And second, I think that there is the cultural dimension that is not being evoked. It is true that Islamic finance, by itself, might be a very good solution, but after all, it is a very particular alternative finance because it is a religious finance. It is based on religious principles, and in a world, especially in Europe, where people and societies have strived for centuries to define secularism, I don't know how easy it will be to implement Islamic finance. Thank you.

de Anca: Thank you. My non-expert opinion would be, why not both? Why does it have to be one or the other? I think that we can all live together with different principles and values, and probably learn from each other. But this is a non-expert answer, so I would like to give the floor to the experts.

Fernández: First, on the ethical issue of my colleague and neighbour here, I was young at some point, and I attended a seminar by the European Union Youth Foundation. Way back in the seventies, so most of you weren't born then! The seminar was called Human Values for Human Kind, and we decided, the outcome, was that we don't need common human values to be able to understand each other. If we insist on fighting over finding common values, we may have a problem. And that is my approach. We really do not need to share many things to be able to live together. Which brings me to banking. We don't need to respect or believe the same ethical values to be able to work together. In fact, the Lebanese journalist said something that I had in my mind. We are all talking about limiting the growth of the balance sheet, and Ignacio made a point, and certainly from what I am learning today, Islamic banking has it in its basic code. The Germans also had it in their basic code. Remember, the Bundesbank was all about limiting credit growth. I know it is not very popular these days to defend the Germans in Europe; it is sort of a German-bashing period, but maybe they were right. Maybe the Bundesbank had a point when they insisted on having monetary policy based on monetary aggregates and on limiting credit growth. Maybe the whole basic idea of M3 and credit growth wasn't just a German obsession after the World War, but has some economic rationale to it, and I personally do believe that this is the case, and it would be an easy way to limit the growth of the balance sheet. So, maybe redefining the rules of monetary policy is a necessary thing to do, maybe not to avoid the next financial crisis, but certainly to make it less imminent and less dramatic.

And then, on the issue of the Islamic banks not having any CDSs or any securities, let me just give you a very sad example of a story. Spanish banks had no securities on their balance sheet, and that did not prevent us from having a serious financial crisis. We just had a lot of land, which was of no real value as a physical asset. So, it would be very good for the Spaniards if there was a necessary correlation between having securities, these CDSs, CDOs, all these strange things, on the balance sheet and crisis, but it just didn't work that way in Spain, unfortunately.

Elgari: Even Islamic banks that have a lot of real estate on their balance sheet are facing problems. It is not a panacea.

I didn't want to leave you with the impression that I disagree with everything the doctor says, so I am going to agree with him on one thing. He said, in that part of the world there are savings that we need to tap. Fine. That's very good. He also said that, if people want to deal this way, fair enough, we have to deal with it, that's fine. But actually we have grandiose hopes of using this opportunity. Of course, Spain is coming rather late to this, because we have had some other 'tappers' of these savings for a quarter of a century now. But welcome! There are still vacant seats. We want to seize this opportunity to really create a lasting relationship. The crisis should be, itself, an opportunity where, yes, we have a lot of savings, and yes, we have preferences that we will make these savings available through Islamic means. That's fine, we all agree on that, but this should not be the end of the story. We want it to be really the meeting of two civilisations; we want it to be a lasting relationship that is beneficial for both nations. And we can all live with our own ethics, but I assure you we have so much in common.

[*applause*]

Hussein Hassan, Deutsche Bank: My name is Hussein Hassan. I work for Deutsche Bank. I just wanted to make a couple of points and maybe ask the audience one question.

Elgari: Ask the audience?

Hassan: Yes, because some of the comments left me a little bit disturbed. I think what we should be looking at is talking about what we can learn in terms of ideas and forget about the Islamic tag. Let's talk about ethical financing, and I wonder whether we would have the same issues about this being not culturally acceptable in Europe. Its idea is, 'Look at the reality. If it is true, apply it.' Don't look at what the justification for it is. And the other point I wanted to raise is that I think we are making a little bit too much of credit growth links to assets. That is not what Islamic finance is about. Islamic finance is about risk participation. It is about financing productivity. So, the question I have to the professor is, would you have the same concern about valuation of assets if we were talking about doing due diligence on financing projects? The asset doesn't have to be in existence. Actually, Islamic finance is not about doing metal commodity warrants. No, it's about financing productivity projects. Do you have the same concerns about valuation in that scenario?

de Anca: I'm afraid, Fernando, you will have to answer.

Fernández: Sure, I have the same concerns, yes. We have the same concerns over the valuation of projects, and there are plenty of projects that have been over-valued, and the expected stream of income coming from those projects being positively correlated with the 'financial folly', the financial boom and the 'animal spirits' that I mentioned. So, unfortunately, the way I see it, I may be wrong, is that the fundamental valuation problem does not disappear, even in project finance.

de Anca: I'm sorry. Very, very quick.

Shaher Abbas, IFAAS, UK: Shaher Abbas from IFAAS, UK. Two things, very quickly. Professor Fernando mentioned that there is maybe no difference between storing value, or holding value, in money and in land. There is a lot of difference, and I am not an economist. The least you can say is about inflation – one will go down, and one will go up. That's the least you can say about the difference in storing value.

The second thing is in reference to, for example, mortgages. When Islamic banks go into mortgages, they go into partnership. The fact that they go into partnership will actually make a lot of difference in terms of the valuation, even if it was a project. In the case that the value of the project is going down, the bank usually cannot get out; and it is not a debt relationship, it is a partnership relationship. So, the value of the holding and the asset value will go down. The whole cycle of what will happen usually in a conventional situation will not happen. All the defaults, all the selling of the houses and the complete cycle of what happens after the defaults will not happen in Islamic finance. Thank you very much.

de Anca: Thank you. Now I think it is time to close the door. But before closing, I would like first, Dr Chapra, if you want to react to the discussions, and then probably a word from each of the members of the table to close the debate.

Chapra: Well, the fact is that Islamic finance is not something new. The name 'Islamic finance', it would have been better if it was not used, because a number of the principles of Islamic finance are a part of the Western tradition also. And, when we say, 'Islamic finance', we drive many people away from it. So, if it was, as one of the commentators said, 'ethical finance', maybe it might have been a better term to use, and it would have been more acceptable.

So, conventional finance has made a great deal of contribution to the development of the world, and there are a number of things we can learn from conventional finance, and they have been incorporated in Islamic finance to a great extent. And there are principles of Islamic finance which conventional finance can take and, I think, reduce the possibility of crises in the financial system. Of course, this doesn't mean that crises will never take place. Crises are a part of life. All we can do is reduce their severity and frequency. Some of the principles of Islamic finance can help in this. If these principles are adopted, I think that conventional finance would be stronger and more stable and able to contribute to the development of the world in a better way. Thank you.

de Anca: Now, to close the panel, I would like each of the members of the panel to make a very quick last remark. Ignacio, you start, since Fernando, on my right side, didn't allow you to talk very much.

de la Torre: On the one hand, I fully agree that when we are talking about Islamic finance, it also has some Western roots. It is in the Christian gospel, some words of Jesus Christ saying that it is forbidden to lend with interest. So it was in the Christian tradition until the thirteenth century. In the thirteenth century, the Catholic Church allowed interest to be applied, and this is exactly, Fernando, where the '800 years of financial folly' starts. Take into account that sometimes Islamic finance has to do with non-Muslims. If you look at who really buys the *sukuk*, one of the main buyers of the *sukuk* being issued – for instance, in Dubai – are the Japanese pension funds, even US hedge funds. In the end, there is a lot of non-Islamic investment based on Islamic financial assets.

Also, I think it is a wrong perception to think that Islamic finance is shielded from the crisis. We have already had several defaults of *sukuk*, starting with a US one from East Cameron Partners, a *sukuk* of Nakheel sponsored by the Dubai government, a *sukuk* in Saudi Arabia investing in Kuwait. So, some *sukuk* are going into default, so this is not a magical solution, even though there are some very interesting lessons to be learned.

And finally, I would just like to raise a point that Saudi Arabia opened a stock market for *sukuk*; I think it is called the *Tadawul*, although it doesn't have a lot of listed instruments yet. Also, Madrid would love to have some *sukuk* listed on the Madrid Stock Exchange, and it is hoped that in the future, if we are able to make some transactions, some of these will be listed either in Riyadh or Madrid.

de Anca: Fernando, last remarks, quickly.

Fernández: First of all, it may have been in the thirteenth century when the '800 years of financial folly' started, but that is also when nominal GDP and GDP per capita made a huge difference. So there is, unfortunately – well for me, maybe for you fortunately – a relationship between the development of the financial sector and the level of human social development in the world. And this is a fact. You only have to look at GDP per capita to see what happened afterwards.

On the profit-sharing concept that was mentioned a couple of times. It sounds very attractive, but the last time we tried it, it was called 'industrial banks', and we have a problem with industrial banks. It so happened that when banks in the Western world had significant personal involvement and capital involvement in the real sector by owning industrial firms, it didn't work very well. It actually increased the volatility and the credit procyclicality of the financial system.

However, having said this, I still firmly believe what I said at the beginning, and I firmly believe that we do not have to share all values, attitudes or financial regulations to be able to work together. And I firmly believe that the world is a safer and better place for all of us if we are able to find common ground and not dispute over the differences that will always be with us. And there is common ground here. There is a pool of savings, and the professor mentioned before that a lot of people have tapped it already, that we are late. But we are used to being late. We've always been late. That doesn't change things. It is an opportunity, it is an additional source of financing, I do agree also that ....

[*break in recording*]

... through the whole European economic environment, what we now call the European Union, was based on this idea that we are doing business together, you become closer socially, culturally, politically, humanly. So this is not an alien concept to the European tradition, on the contrary. So, we don't disagree that much, and we may even be able to do business together.

de Anca: Dr Elgari.

Elgari: Of course, you are keeping the best for last, right?

[*laughter*]

I just want to reiterate what Dr Chapra has just mentioned. Actually, a friend of mine, a former Professor of Business at Harvard Business School – of course, being so old all my friends are former – who was actually quite interested and was consulting many Islamic banks, said, 'Islamic banking is a superior form of banking. Too bad you called it Islamic.'

I said, 'Why?'

And he said, 'Because when you called it "Islamic", you actually blinded our eyes for making a judgement on the merits of the system.'

And I agree with my friend that if we just give these ideas an opportunity to be evaluated on their own merits, believe me, they make a lot of sense. Thank you very much.

de Anca: Thank you all for being here.

[*applause*]

2
Introduction to Islamic Economics and Finance

Symposium workshop

IE Business School, Madrid, Spain, 17 June 2010

Chairmen

Dr Ibrahim Aboulola, Deputy Director, Islamic Economics Research
Centre, King Abdulaziz University, Saudi Arabia
Prof. José Collado Medina, Economics and Business Faculty,
Universidad Nacional de Educación a Distancia, Spain

Special Comments

Prof. Umer Chapra, Advisor, Islamic Development Bank, Saudi Arabia

What is Islamic economics? What is the common ground between Islamic economics and traditional economics?

Islamic economics is based on the principles and norms for human
welfare derived from Islamic sources. Fundamentally different from
the secularly defined system, it offers a comprehensive and coherent
alternative to conventional, or Western, economics. There are many
similarities and much common ground between Islamic economics
and Western economics – for example, the question of allocation
and distribution of resources, the fulfilment of material needs and

the importance of the market mechanism. Islamic finance does not seek to abolish private property, nor does it attempt to prevent the individual from serving his own self-interest. The emphasis of Islamic economics, however, is a concentration on human brotherhood and social economic justice. While it recognises the role of the market in the efficient allocation of resources, it does not find competition to be a sufficient safeguard of social interests. Moreover, based on a religious world view, Islamic economics incorporates a belief in 'the day of the hereafter', something which renders a great many of the theories of traditional Western economics unacceptable.

With respect to the common ground between the two philosophies, had it not been for the secular influence of the Enlightenment movement in Europe, Western economics today, as an evolution of the pre-Enlightenment Judeo-Christian world view, might not have been significantly different from Islamic economics. That is not to say that all Western economists abandoned their moral values to become materialists or social Darwinists, since many retained their religious world view.

It is notable that the West has enjoyed a very long period of prosperity in market-orientated economies; however, it has failed to eliminate poverty and fulfil the needs of all members of society. Inequality of income and wealth continues, as does a substantial degree of economic instability, including the current economic crisis and unemployment. Throughout Western economic development and its phenomenal rise in wealth, efficiency and equity have remained elusive.

It is important to bear in mind, when referring to conventional economics, that it is not a homogeneous discipline, as it is sometimes portrayed by Islamic economists. It contains differing points of view, which is something that is often overlooked when criticising conventional economics. While being predominantly secular, Western economics benefits from the contributions of economists who were, to a greater or lesser degree, more morally orientated. A number of well-known economists over the years have criticised the materialist and secular culture and endeavoured to inject the moral point of view into conventional economics.

One must be careful, therefore, when comparing conventional economics to its Islamic counterpart, not to fall into the trap of considering that Western economics is a completely unified, homogeneous philosophy and that its secular, materialist nature implies that it is devoid of moral principles. This interpretation of conventional economics as lacking value judgements comes from the fact that freedom gains a greater importance under a secular regime. Freedom exists also under a religious system, but within the framework of moral guidelines. In the secular West, the individual ought to be completely free from such restrictions. However, this is often not the case, since all economists are working within a cultural framework which they cannot escape.

In the West, Christian values were quite pervasive and impacted society quite widely, which is why you see that the Western world, as a whole, has greater justice and greater moral ethics. In Western countries, democratic governments enforced many Christian values, and those values dominated society, allowing them to make a great deal of progress in all aspects of life. However, with the increasing power of secularism in the West, one can see a rise in a number of problems: for example, family disintegration, which did not exist previously.

There has been more justice and a stronger ethical framework in the West than in the Islamic world. Even though Islamic moral values are spoken about a great deal, the lack of democracy has meant that they are not enforced. There is a *hadith* from the Prophet that states that God enforces the *Qur'an* through the ruler. Since the rulers had no interest in this, but rather in their own luxury, moral principles were not applied in Muslim cultures as they were in the West. Although the Islamic principles exist, they are not observed, and there is no authority to enforce them.

This is an important point; criticism of conventional economics is often based on the assumption that it is totally secular and materialist. But even today this is not the case, despite Western moral principles having weakened over the years. On the whole, if you look at it, many things in the Western world are better today than in the Muslim world.

One possible definition of economics is 'the science of human action under the conditions of scarcity'. That human action has two components. The first is the goals, objectives, norms and values for which one strives. The second part is how they are achieved. That is the technical part. In the early development of conventional economics, there was no doubt about what people should strive for; values were settled. What was lacking was an understanding of what was happening, in markets, for example.

This offers some reason for why Western economics has tended to focus on positive economics, that part of economics that concerns itself with observing and explaining economic behaviour and theories. It should be noted, however, that for early economists (Adam Smith, for example), it still contained both components: positive economics and normative economics, which focuses on norms and values. As traditional economics emerged, since there was no lack of value judgements, but a lack of explanations, some economists, for example Max Weber, forcibly argued for concentrating on the positive dimension of economics, although it should be noted he also argued strongly that the normative should not be neglected.

With recourse to facts and empirical data, there are many methodologies to analyse positive economic issues, but Western economists are not trained to tackle the normative aspect, since that has been largely neglected. Since the 1960s secular economics has gone even further, with critical rationalism becoming the mainstream economic methodology, and Karl Popper even narrowing down the discipline to not only the positive elements, but an empirical science. Thus, Western economists are ill prepared to enter into a dialogue with Muslim economists, who emphasise strongly the normative dimension.

While the basic values are actually quite similar, the implications have been different, for example, in their enforcement. However, this has been less of a concern in Western society for the last few decades, or even the last two centuries, since the idea of separating the power to enforce things and the individual's moral education, the idea of not imposing a normative consensus, has been important. So, the history of economic thought took different directions, which clouds the debate, despite so many shared values. Perhaps now there is a convergence once again. To whom has the normative debate been left? Philosophers? Religious people? Politicians, basically. This may not have been a wise decision, since the system today resembles sheer pragmatism and not much talk of values. Comparing the ideals of one political party, such as can be found in any manifesto, with actual politics, it is hard to believe it represents the same group of people. So, politicians also tend to lose sight of the systemic implications and are no better qualified to enter the normative discussion. More and more economists are, once again, starting to criticise governments and the inconsistencies in their goals and objectives.

There is a gap that conventional economists must bridge, to re-learn how to enter into a debate about values and systemic preferences, in order to facilitate a meaningful dialogue with their Islamic counterparts, who, unlike the West, use the approach of normative economics as a starting point. This may be strange in Western economics, but since the normative aspect no longer appears to be functioning properly, this needs to be addressed, and it appears to be happening.

The dichotomy between secular thinking and moral principles has really sharpened in the last three decades with the growth of the financial sector, specifically its autonomous growth decoupled from the productive sector. This trend started around the time of the governments of President Reagan in the US and Prime Minister Thatcher in the UK. Political leaders seeking a justification for this kind of economics found it in economists like Michael Nowak, who actually justified the removal of value-based economics on religious grounds, on the basis that value creation, not moral values, was the first priority. The distribution of that created value, which is the correct domain for those moral judgements, would be taken care of by the markets, since interfering in the distributional aspects would only create a mess. This was the excuse the financial sector needed to support its expansion.

The present crisis shows that the assumptions on which that model was built, that the creation of economic value should be the first objective, and that the distribution of that economic benefit will be managed by the market, are deeply flawed. With asset bubbles and so forth, it appears that the market cannot be relied upon, and the role of the state will need to be reinstated. However, the state is not necessarily the ideal entity to discharge that role.

One of the problems is that, when economists speak to Islamic scholars, the scholars say that the state should be responsible for the collection and the distribution of *zakah* and enforce social equity. However, when asked about the experience of the state in Muslim countries for the last 40 years, they go silent, because that experience has been problematic to say the least.

Now, in the post-crisis period, the arrogance that has been shown by conventional economics is somewhat diminished, as it can no longer claim to have all the answers. Perhaps with this increased humility there is some room to reintroduce the distributional equity aspects. There is tension now in Western countries where budgets are constrained and cuts are inevitable. One of the first assaults is on the welfare state and state benefits. How those cuts are realised, and who will bear their burden, will depend on the values of those societies. Will it fall disproportionately on the poor, or will it be shared equitably?

These are the questions that Muslim economists should address. It is no good to claim to espouse distributional equity if it cannot be linked to the Islamic instruments that have been developed. That will not close the gap with conventional economics. However, addressing together the common agenda of distributional equity may achieve it.

In defence of secular economics and its approach to values in economics, one of the major contributions in the area of normative economics and social justice is that of agency theory – the Nobel Prize for Economics being awarded to Spence, Stiglitz and Akerlof for their work in this field. It is a theory that has been developing since the 1970s, and it deals, in a purely secular way, with human conflicts and how human conflicts can be resolved.

Both Islamic and Western finance can agree that many instances have been witnessed of managerial abuses of power; individuals pursuing their own self-interest to the detriment of the interests of the shareholders. This is not fair and does not increase equity. Both sides can agree on that, and religiously derived values or principles are not necessary to resolve that issue. Mechanisms from agency theory have also evolved into other fields of research, such as corporate governance, which directly address how to resolve this issue. Managers' compensation and monitoring, by corporate boards, for instance, are highly practical considerations coming from that normative body of secular economics started by professors who first dealt with those questions of moral hazard and agency theory in general.

These are the relevant questions which have been identified by academia and are being applied in practice to corporate governance, and not those crisis issues that today dominate the attention of politicians, managers and businessmen. This is evidence of how, from a secular point of view, based on conventional economic paradigms, values can be handled in a purely secular world.

When discussing Islamic economics and finance, there is often a tendency for the conversation to shift immediately to the financial aspects. However, it is important to address the main interests of Islamic economics, since without that foundation it would be very difficult to manage the financial world.

It appears that what today is referred to as 'Islamic finance' has not benefited from the foundation of Islamic economics as a moral economy, because it has not been developed properly from those core principles. In its attempt to be competitive, Islamic finance has positioned itself quite closely to conventional finance; therefore, it is important to make the distinction between Islamic economics and conventional economics. This does not imply a radical departure or political positioning. However, the difference is important, and that difference is in the value system, the moral dimension.

Perhaps the term 'economics' is problematic when discussing the moral, or value-orientated, economy. There have been a number of secular economists who have made important contributions to moral economics. However, they often do not define themselves according to a traditional, neoclassical, marginalist theory. It may be helpful, therefore, to position Islamic economics more in the context of an eighteenth-century perspective on political economy, similar to that of Adam Smith, for instance, through which it would become possible to internalise values in the system. Consider those secular contributors to the development of a moral economy, for example Amartya Sen and Amitai Etzioni: they associate themselves more with that tradition of economics, rather than a narrowly defined neoclassical approach.

The definition of conventional economics as it stands today is a product of that marginalist movement of the early twentieth century, excluding from the analysis not only values, but also institutions. Thus, it fails, one way or another, to provide a comprehensive understanding of economic problems and how to respond to them.

Returning to the perspective of political economy, such as in the recent trends in secular economics towards institutional economics and cultural economics, for example, reintroducing those missing elements in economics analysis may be the solution to this problem. This is the perspective of Islamic economics. In Islamic economics, that political economy aspect must be identified and must make direct reference to those value judgements, which are considered divine in essence.

With the development of an economics that includes a diversity of approaches, there is certainly a place for Islamic economics. It is not a radical departure, since many of the elements of Islamic finance have been seen before in the contributions of secular economists like John Stuart Mill or Joseph Schumpeter. The difference is that Islamic economics does not share so much with that part of conventional economics as a science of human behaviour under conditions of scarcity, whereas from the point of view of political economy, which internalises value judgements, there is immense common ground. Western economists coming from that political economic background will find they can engage easily with Islamic economics, more so that those from the narrowly defined neoclassical version of economics, who dismiss not only Islamic economics but all form of value-orientated economics.

Therefore, redefining Islamic economics as Islamic political economy, there is plenty of scope for Islamic economists to work with their secular counterparts, and Islamic economics can easily be located within a heterogeneous economic tradition and make a significant contribution towards internalising value judgements into secular economics.

What is the 'Great Gap Theory'? How realistic is it? Relate the issue to Spanish heritage

In his *History of Economic Analysis*, published in 1954, four years after his death, Joseph Schumpeter wrote that the period between the Greeks and the Scholastics was sterile and unproductive. This concept, referred to as the 'Great Gap Theory', has become ingrained in conventional economics. However, when examining the 600 years to which Schumpeter was referring, one can discover the emergence and evolution of many 'modern' theories treating, for example, property rights, the division of labour and specialisation, the importance of saving and investment for development, the roles of both supply and demand in determining prices and the factors that affect them, the role of money and exchange, the market mechanism, counterfeiting, currency debasement, Gresham's law, the development of cheques, letters of credit, labour supply and population, the role of the state, justice, peace and stability and development. Of particular note are the contributions of Ibn Khaldun and others to the principles of taxation. Professor Abdul Azim Islahi is one of the scholars who have written about this subject, and he pinpoints very clearly the contributions of Muslims in this period.

In the case of Ibn Khaldun, his contribution was so significant that many of the things he said were stated again by Keynes in the twentieth century. Even some of the remarks of Professor Sen were indicated by great Muslim scholars centuries beforehand.

Science advances through the many small contributions of different individuals, and these contributions have also come from the Muslim world. The Western economists who have repeated those assertions may have been borrowing directly from those Islamic scholars of antiquity, or they may have been unaware of them, but that does not diminish the contributions of Islamic economists throughout history. In light of this, the Great Gap Theory cannot be supported and subsequently is not such a popular theory today. It is necessary, therefore, to rewrite the history of economic analysis, paying due attention to the insights of Islamic economists.

Schumpeter's economic Great Gap Theory is sometimes seen as part of a larger Great Gap scenario in the Western perspective. There seems to be a feeling that when Europe entered the Dark Ages, Greek and Roman knowledge passed to the Muslims, where it was preserved in translation, kept safe, and then somehow handed back completely in re-translation, via places like Spain, for example, without those guardians having impacted it. That is the essence of the Great Gap Theory – that there is a discontinuity from Greek and Roman times to the modern era and that there was little or no advancement of knowledge in that intervening period. And it is not restricted to economics but is found also in science and other disciplines. Of course, acknowledging that intervening period would mean accommodating the learning gained in the Islamic world.

In economics in particular, you find two important developments from the Muslim world that have proved critical to the development of commerce. One is the invention of the number system that is in use today and algebra, while the other is book-keeping and the meticulous recording of transactions that is the precursor to modern-day accounting. Commerce could not have flourished without these advances, which go to show that the Great Gap Theory of economics is untenable. Nevertheless, it remains part of the larger, civilisational debate that needs to be addressed.

This may not be an innocent case of missing the economic discourse that has been conducted in other parts of the world, but perhaps is due to the larger philosophical issue of the Eurocentric perception of creating knowledge. From that perspective, unfortunately, knowledge created outside of the period of the Enlightenment, and the Enlightenment societies, is not recognised in the main body of knowledge. Edward Said, at the same time as deconstructing the Orientalist view, showed how Eurocentric perspectives are imposed on other societies while failing to recognise their contributions.

So, the Great Gap Theory is a result of that exclusion of ideas and knowledge created beyond the realm of the Enlightenment and is not limited to Muslim societies but fails to recognise the achievements of many other cultures also, since they were considered stagnant, non-modern societies; thus, no knowledge creation could take place there. It would be necessary, therefore, to embrace a renewed attitude with respect to knowledge development, going beyond the Eurocentric perspective and knowledge base and accepting the knowledge created by any culture as an equally valid contribution to human civilisation. This is a civilisational issue, beyond simple economic methodology, and should be addressed.

The importance of Islamic political economy, or Islamic moral economy, is that it is a clear challenge to that Eurocentric perspective. It is an alternative knowledge base, with its own institutions – that is, the culmination of centuries' worth of experience and study. It is a great response to the Great Gap Theory, which endures, since Islamic economics and finance struggle to gain a foothold in business schools in the Western world.

What is the role of moral values in Islamic economics?

The emphasis of conventional economics lies in behaviour, respecting the tastes and preferences of individuals. Islamic finance, on the other hand, places emphasis on individual and social reform through moral uplift, modifying human behaviour, tastes and preferences. As a complement to the price mechanism, intended to promote general well-being, those guiding Islamic morals form a moral filter through which individuals are expected to pass their claims on resources. This process endeavours to eliminate conspicuous consumption and excessive claims on resources by individuals.

Conventional economics relies solely on the price mechanism to allocate resources, with excess claims on the goods and services being kept in check by higher prices. This mechanism of limiting the access to those goods and services is more restrictive for the poor than for the rich. Islamic economics, on the other hand, introduces the moral mechanism alongside the price mechanism, so that some of the excess demand for goods and services is eliminated before turning to the market, and a lower equilibrium price is achieved. The effect is a more equitable result in Islamic finance as it establishes a situation that permits greater access to resources for a large section of society.

What is permitted or prohibited in Islamic finance is defined in the *Shari'a* instructions. There are two sides to those instructions; where they pertain to worship they provide great detail, even too much detail, but where they pertain to human behaviour, they are more flexible. With respect to the question of buying and selling, and economics and finance in general, the *Shari'a* instructions permit Muslims to do everything that is not specifically prohibited: for example, *riba*, usury or interest, *gharar* or uncertainty, and such things. As a result, just a few rules can control human behaviour, which makes Islamic finance more flexible than is generally perceived. Therefore, it can be implemented in many places worldwide and at different times.

One important consideration of Islamic finance regarding human behaviour is best serving the interests of individuals versus the interests of the wider community. When considering the question of how to invest one's money, a conventional interest-bearing investment may be the preferred option for the individual investor. However, it may not necessarily be so favourable for society as a whole. One example of this may be the borrower who suffers a setback and is not able to meet their repayments, in which case the contract benefits the lender with a guaranteed return on investment but does so at the expense of the hardship the borrower faces in being obliged to meet the repayments.

Of the moral values that are intrinsic to Islamic finance, the removal of poverty and how the system reacts to poverty is perhaps the most important. The Islamic principle of *zakah*, alms-giving or charity, is specifically targeted to the task of removing poverty. This is not intended to equalise people but to reduce the gap between the rich and the poor. It is not against the differences with which everyone has been created, but aims to remove differences that are extravagant or exaggerated. This is achieved through *zakah*, *sadaqah* and other means. Of course, it is still possible to see the very, very rich and the very, very poor; however, Islamic principles oblige Muslims to strive for greater equality.

It has been said that if one scratches an economist, any economist, underneath one will find morals. Economics studies human behaviour, and that behaviour will necessarily be influenced by embedded moral values. Thus, it is conceivable that all economics is value-loaded, the difference being the source of those values. In Western economics, values and morals do exist and are usually referred to as ethics. However, these ethics are usually more personal rather than defined by society. The comparison of conventional versus Islamic economics is actually the comparison of secular versus religiously derived values. This implies that the secular perspective is actually possessed of its own value structure, which is enshrined in capitalism and the market, and that these are not, of themselves, natural phenomena but rather the result of conscious intervention and the value biases which that implies.

Most people think that Islamic economics is about the elimination of interest from the economy, that this is the most important goal as it is stated in the *Qur'an*. This is a practical consideration of Islamic economics, but the moral values that should be expressed through this alternative model of economics have greater importance than the merely practical. That is not to say that such practical considerations are not important and may be dismissed, but they are present in support of the higher moral objective of ensuring equality and the equitable distribution of resources in society.

Many tools have been developed to facilitate this. However, the integration of these practical tools is where Islamic finance must begin to interface with its Western counterparts. It is important to address questions such as: What is *murabaha* or *musharaka*? What is partnership? How are debts to be dealt with? If interest is not permitted, how is it possible to do business with companies that deal with interest? These are questions on which much work has been done by Islamic economists, and there exists a great opportunity now to introduce these things. However, by first addressing these practical things, it may be easier for the West to embrace these elements of Islamic finance, rather than discussing the more theoretical aspects.

With respect to practical considerations, one question that should be addressed by Islamic scholars is how Islamic economics can be presented to students alongside conventional economics. A typical case study to use would be that of investing in bonds for the purpose of funding one's children's education, for instance. By going to the market and buying a risk-free government bond, one can receive the principal plus interest at the time it is needed, when the children go to university. Few would argue that this is not a legitimate moral objective, so it is not a question of conspicuous consumption. It is a decision regarding how one's consumption is allocated between now and the future.

From a conventional finance point of view this is a perfectly valid way of addressing the consumption of a given good, in this case, education. However, there is nothing tangible being transferred in these transactions, no physical asset available to back the deal; thus, it would appear that such a transaction would not be feasible in Islamic finance. If Islamic finance requires some form of profit-sharing in order to realise a return, how can this be achieved? In such a scenario, what incentives exist for individuals to save for future consumption?

Bonds and securities are not the only way of investing for the future. Research published in the *American Economic Journal* has shown that the rate of return on securities over the last 100 years has been just one percent, whereas equity has returned seven percent. In the short-term, a defined rate of interest may offer a higher return, but in the long run, investing in equity has been more profitable. Moreover, equity offers the prospect of capital gains, which is not the case with a bond, and the value of the bond may be adversely affected by changes in the interest rate.

Of course, investing in equity is expected to offer a higher return, since it carries a higher risk. There are some savings for which the investor does not want to assume that level of risk, for instance, in the case of someone who is approaching retirement. Thus, in conventional finance the standard practice for those approaching retirement is to move their investments from equity into bonds, in order to reduce their risk as their capacity to absorb financial setbacks is diminished by the impending cessation of a regular income. A saving scenario that is reliant on equity investments will therefore be overloaded with risk, compared to an interest-based issue. Since investing for one's future retirement is a fundamental question for the vast majority of individuals and governments in Western societies, there is a big question of how pension plans under Islamic finance would approach this kind of situation.

Islamic funds are one alternative. There are two main types: equity-based *musharaka* and sale-based *mudaraba*, which will ensure the return of the principal. Of course, the consumer will not manage the investment in these types of instruments personally; they will be bought and sold by the bank as usual. Just as with a conventional bank, the money is invested in an account with an Islamic bank, which then does its business, buying and selling their various contracts, either *salam, istisna'a* or *murabaha*, and this will almost guarantee the principal plus a return.

Many Islamic banks in Saudi Arabia are doing this, for precisely that education-based reason. Everyone is concerned about the future of their children and would like to have some savings for the provision of their higher education. The arrangement that the bank makes is to create a fund, of which everyone is able to purchase a share with some fairly modest payments, perhaps just €100, or even €50, per month. This creates a pool of money which is then invested in some sort of semi-secured investment or project, and it is the responsibility of the bank managing the fund to ensure that the risk – the possibility of a loss – is minimal. Even though the profit may be very small, the idea is not to make a profit but to have some savings and ensure a bright future for the children. This is not something theoretical but is in place and being offered by banks to hundreds of thousands of people who are using this service. The schemes exist for terms from two to three years or for much longer periods. The Islamic banks can utilise the money in more or less risky investments, using *mudaraba, murabaha, salam, istisna'a, wakalah* or whatever, and at the end of the period there will be a return. It may be minimal, but in the long term there will be a real profit.

Research has indicated that the returns on equity are significantly higher than the returns on the corresponding interest-based investments. Interest-based investments are not the only solution for saving for the future of one's children, and Islamic finance has many different ways of investing in equity. The short-term variation in equity is great, but in the long run it is more profitable and would appear to be a better way to save for that future.

However, what is clear is that people have differing attitudes to risk, and even a single person may have different attitudes to risk at different times throughout his or her life. The theory says that having the option to invest in more or less risky assets, that is, to have a 'complete market' in economic terminology, is going to lead to a better allocation of resources than if one channel is removed: for example, the less risky, interest-based investments. Islamic finance appears to follow that route, prohibiting the use of those low-risk, interest-based instruments, thus obliging all investors to carry a higher level of risk, which is less efficient and not the optimal solution for everyone, nor for anyone at a given point in time.

If an Islamic bank is investing in truly Islamic contracts, which implies profit and loss sharing, there is clearly an element of risk involved. If the same bank is then offering savers risk-free, or close to risk-free, Islamic products because consumers are demanding them, that implies a transfer of risk from the investors, the savers, to the banks themselves. This would appear to be a problem for the banks, which then face the question of how they will be able to cover that risk.

One theory posited as to how Islamic banks mitigate that risk is through their size. Unlike individuals, banks are involved in a large number of different transactions, so although they may experience some losses, overall they should realise a significant profit and thus offset those loss-making investments against the majority of profitable investments. Thus, the size of banks allows them to mitigate risk through diversification, far more so than individuals can.

The way to invest Islamically that will minimise the risk is not based on profit- and loss-sharing, but rather on sale-based contracts, which almost guarantee the principal and a return. So-called *murabaha* contracts are a form of debt that can be secured by the bank, protecting the principal and the return, so the risk is minimal. The actual risk is just slightly higher than interest-based investments because of some technicalities regarding defaults and such things, but the risk can come very close to that offered by conventional banks. Islamic finance offers an array of contracts and ways to invest, offering different potential returns and risks. The two main categories are equity-based and sale-based; equity-based being the more risky, higher-return profit- and loss-sharing investments and sale-based contracts, like *murabaha*, *salam* and *istisna'a*, representing a lower risk option.

Even though Islamic finance does, in certain circumstances, carry a higher burden of risk than some forms of conventional finance, this also has a positive social effect. In a profit- and loss-sharing contract where the investor, in the role of a lender, is also exposed to the risk, those lenders become more cautious in their choice of investments. As a result Islamic finance leads to greater responsibility and professionalism from the finance industry.

It is interesting to compare Western and Islamic economics with respect to three main points: consumption, saving and investment. Regarding consumption, Islamic economists claim that Muslims have healthier habits compared to Western consumers, who are liable to spend a lot of money on useless things based on the encouragement of the advertising industry. Clearly, not everyone is so heavily influenced, and it depends largely on the individual. Saving does not appear to be very different between the two economies, which leaves just investment as the main point of difference.

The Islamic investor is inclined to think deeply before making an investment whether that investment complies with his moral code and the values that have been passed to him through the teachings of his religion. The Western investor, on the other hand, only really begins to become concerned after the investment has been made; that is to say, his concern is that the investment, once initiated, is managed ethically according to the accepted codes of conduct.

Another very important point is the role of interest rates and their role in monetary policy. The interest rate is the main lever of monetary policy in Western economies. However, if this control is eliminated, as in Islamic countries, the only possibility remaining is to monitor monetary aggregates in order to avoid them becoming inflationary. Thus, in conventional economics, there are two mechanisms available to control monetary policy, while Islamic economics has just one.

Despite the absence of interest rates as a way to manage monetary policy, Islamic economics still has some tools available: the legal reserve issues, open market operations and the pressure that the central bank can apply in directing policy. As a result, Islamic control of monetary policy is usually through buying and selling in open market operations. In certain cases, for instance in Saudi Arabia, physical policies, such as government expenditure, are preferred to direct the economy and thwart the problems of inflation, unemployment and so on.

It is important to note, however, that so-called Islamic countries do not necessarily apply Islamic economics in the management of their central banks. It is therefore not correct to assume that non-interest, *Shari'a*-based, Islamic economics is being used to control monetary policy, even in Islamic countries. In fact, very few central banks are using *Shari'a*-compliant instruments to direct monetary policy.

There is a difference between Muslim countries and Islamic economics. This is because Islamic economics presents a theoretical model which is by no means broadly applied. Where it is practised, it can be described as a niche market. In the financial sector, it is just ten to fifteen percent of the market; in some countries twenty-five percent, but that is really the exception.

There is, however, an instrument that could essentially evolve into something similar to the interest rate control mechanism of Western finance, and that is *sukuk*. *Sukuk* are de facto Islamic bonds, behaving very similarly to interest-bearing bonds, but legally are an equity instrument. The *sukuk* holder is a partial owner of real assets that are leased to a bankruptcy remote lessee. One common example is that of the Saxony-Anhalt tax office. The buildings that house the tax office of this German state were transferred to a Special Purpose Vehicle, shares of which were sold off to the *sukuk* holders. The SPV then leases the buildings back to the Saxony-Anhalt tax department, generating an income stream, which is then returned to the *sukuk* certificate holders, who are joint owners of the buildings. This then has the appearance of a triple-A, quasi-interest-bearing bond. Such an instrument, further developed, could be a useful benchmark for pricing other Islamic finance products.

This type of *sukuk* is an attractive prospect for many central banks as a way to address a serious problem in Islamic banking: liquidity management. Short-term possibilities to place, or get liquidity when needed, could be served by this type of commercial paper, issued by governments or central banks, meeting all the requirements of *Shari'a* law on the one hand and on the other addressing the commercial needs of the financial community. Central banks would become linked to the capital markets through this type of instrument, which could be something very close, as a benchmark, to interest rates. So, evolving beyond the most basic forms of *murabaha* and other more basic contracts, it is possible to emulate quite effectively the instruments for controlling monetary policy that exist in conventional Western economics.

One element that is missing from the *sukuk* definition in terms of replicating interest-bearing bonds is the question of what happens at the termination of the *sukuk* agreement. In many cases, there is a buy-back agreement, where the issuer agrees to repurchase the assets. When the assets are repurchased at the issue price, or the face value, then the resulting *sukuk* really does replicate a conventional bond.

The hybrid nature of *sukuk* is something that could make it very interesting for Western companies. At first glance, it would qualify as equity, therefore improving the capitalisation of the company, reducing leverage and boosting the credit rating. If, from a legal perspective, however, it is possible to receive a tax deduction for the instalments paid, the quasi-interest payments, it would have the tax benefit of a debt. This type of structure, if feasible, would be very attractive to non-Islamic businesses as well.

One complication for *sukuk* is the transfer of ownership. The legal requirements are often very specific, and it has implications for the *Shari'a* compliance of the instrument also. When creating the SPV, there is the option to transfer into it the full ownership of the physical assets backing the contract, or just the usufruct, that is, the income stream generated and the right to earn money from those assets. This will impact upon the rating the *sukuk* receives. If real, high-quality assets are transferred into the SPV, then the rating may even be higher than for the issuing company, since something has been taken out of the company. If what has been transferred to the *sukuk* is just the usufruct, then the result is essentially a debt relationship against the company issuing the *sukuk*, and the SPV does not own anything on which recourse can be taken in critical cases, so the rating will correspond to the rating of the issuing company, the obligor.

With these two types of *sukuk*, there is much debate over how well each of them complies with *Shari'a* principles. For example, in the case of a buy-back guarantee at the issue price, or in the case of not transferring the full ownership of the assets, there are doubts over the *Shari'a* compliance. There is no simple answer.

However, with respect to benchmarking and monetary policy, what is really of interest are those *sukuk* issued by public authorities, for example, the Central Bank of Bahrain issuing a short-term *sukuk* for liquidity management or the Islamic Development Bank's medium-term *sukuk*. What is missing is a long-term *sukuk* option, which would allow the drawing of a complete yield curve to have benchmarks for all different types of maturities.

To return to the moral issue, theoretically one would expect to see an economic environment in place that would produce in the individuals within that environment a certain type of behaviour. As a result, comparing the behaviour of the 'Islamic agent', inspired by Islamic moral economy, to the conventional economy's 'Western agent', one would expect to observe differences in the habits of the individuals within those cultures in terms of saving and investment. That theoretical expectation would also imply a certain utility function for each, and the Islamic utility function would differ from the neoclassical Western one. The Islamic utility function would have two dimensions, the second being the accountability factor that arises from the Muslim belief in the hereafter.

Looking at the practice in Muslim countries, there is not much of a difference. The hegemony of global forces is too great, and the consumption ethic is that of the individual, regardless of whether he is ethical, or Muslim or Christian. So, that particular theory appears not to work. In fact, it would appear that ethically based financing in the West achieves more than can be seen in the Islamic world. There is room to develop the theory, but the reality does not agree with the theory. The pattern of consumption in Dubai is probably more extravagant than on the streets of Madrid. So, more work is required to establish those models, and even the most basic utility function can be extended, theoretically, to internalise the moral dimension. Islamic political economy has that potential to introduce that moral dimension.

Why do financial crises occur? What is the difference, in explaining the causes and prescribing the solutions, between Islamic economics and traditional views?

This idea of using *sukuk* as an instrument of monetary policy might be related to a case involving the Prophet Muhammad. Having a problem of debt and being in need of resources, Muhammad requested that a member of his family, al-Abbas, his paternal uncle, pay *zakah* in advance for the following two to three years. He thus was able to solve the problem that he had at the time. This shows that, when talking about monetary policy or financial policy, the tools exist, and it is a case of considering them and applying them.

The nature of Islamic finance – investing in particular – appears to be that it prefers certain types of projects, those which are linked to the real economy, particularly real estate and infrastructure. If the financial sector is more closely linked to the real economy, in principle it is true that the periodic, or cyclical, financial crises that arise will be reduced. However, Islamic finance is not investing exclusively in projects related to the real economy, but also in real estate, which has a tendency to be speculative, and thus Islamic banks are participating in real estate 'bubbles', such as happened in Dubai. Thus, it would seem that Islamic economics does not solve the crisis problem as it can be seen to be entering into that cycle.

This leads to the question of how *Shari'a* boards select projects for investment and whether the current economic crisis is leading those *Shari'a* boards to reconsider where investments are being placed and whether there is a discussion about a better way to choose projects for investment, including real estate assets.

The conversation about the application of Islamic economics and finance in the West is usually dominated by discussions of a dichotomy. However, in light of the present financial crisis, and talking about the new financial order, it is important to focus on the complementary aspects. The discussion that matters now involves rethinking the financial and economic models that have worked for the last century.

The preceding discussion regarding risk-loaded equity investments versus low-risk, or risk-free, securities and so forth is very much from a traditional perspective. The experience of the current economic crisis is that by far the riskiest assets were corporate bonds. Looking at the situation in Greece in 2010, one even had to ask whether cash really is risk-free. The conventional system is in a process of reorientation, and it is a reorientation process that is being contributed to not only by Islamic finance but also by the socially responsible investment sector.

The questions arising during this reorientation are largely ethical, and so, from a certain point of view, they share something with Islamic finance and with socially responsible investments (SRIs), but they also go beyond that. Corporate governance is a big issue, and investors are asking questions about how the companies they invest in are being managed. What are the company's labour standards, environmental profile and social responsibility record? The overall discussion, therefore, is not just looking at conventional finance and Islamic finance but also includes SRI as it complements the others very well.

Introducing socially responsible investment into the discussion proves that there is common ground to be explored between Western finance and Islamic finance despite their different value systems.

Socially responsible investing has been using non-financial criteria in the selection of investments around the world for decades. Leverage, the role of assets underlying the transactions and the importance of guarantees were discounted in favour of other criteria which took precedence over pure financial performance. Now the SRI sector, as a subset of Western finance, is pointing to Islamic finance as a discipline from which much can be learned as it addresses many of the issues that have led to the international financial crisis.

Widening the scope a bit, Islamic finance has a lot to offer, even for ethical or socially responsible investing, since this sector has not traditionally addressed issues such as leverage, real assets underlying the contracts, guarantees or profit and loss sharing. The SRI industry now realises that it may have been neglecting certain important financial criteria. The finance industry has shown the importance of leverage, the derivatives markets have highlighted the importance of dealing with real assets, and guarantees are important as they put strain on certain market participants, especially when certain players begin taking on too much risk. This then leads to the 'too big to fail' question. What is to be done with a bank that has accepted so much risk that its failure would be catastrophic for the industry as a whole?

Researchers might refer to this process of re-evaluating conventional economics and finance as a search for a dominant theory, and it really should go beyond looking just at Islamic finance. Islamic finance has established itself and will continue to develop, becoming more important in years to come. However, the SRI sector has also made some interesting developments over the last 40 years and considering it also from a complementary perspective will probably result in a stronger financial industry.

Perhaps it was not so much corporate bonds that were overpriced; rather, other instruments such as CDOs and derivatives clearly were. Surveys of professors from Harvard and MIT have revealed that among their main concerns regarding the future of investments are the structural problems in the bond industry. The industry as it exists today is an oligopoly where a few investment banks make the prices, and this actually led to the liquidity crisis of 2008 to 2009. The losses during that time were much greater on the bond side than on the equity side.

The conventional wisdom is that we have, in order of increasing risk: cash, then government bonds, corporate bonds, hybrid securities and, finally, equities. However, even this needs to be re-thought, since it seems that cash is no longer risk-free, and government debt is increasing. The conventional portfolio theory is therefore in need of revision, and including the lessons of Islamic finance and the SRI sector could result in a more resilient system.

It can appear that, from the point of view of Islamic finance, the principle of having physical assets backing the transactions in some way acts to prevent inflation. Historically, however, there are many examples of unchecked inflation which were due not to excessive leverage but to assets. Examples include Dutch tulips in the seventeenth century, the 'dot-com' bubble or the more recent real-estate bubble in Spain.

In the Spanish real-estate bubble, there were no CDOs, just houses, the prices of which, for a number of reasons, were increasing out of control, but the associated mortgages were never sub-prime, or not to the same degree as in the US. There was no excessive leverage or speculation; however, the asset-backing did not prevent the bubble. The Spanish mortgage industry was not making use of CDOs as was the US market. However, in an increasingly interdependent world, Spain cannot expect to withdraw itself from a general development which has infected the entire industry.

The asset-backed concept, as it is understood in Islamic finance, should not be compared with asset backing in the conventional sense. If the derivatives industry had been asset-backed, the problems of the economic crisis would have been avoided. It simply would not have been possible to create outstanding derivatives worth twelve times the gross national product of the US banking industry.

As an example, in the investment banking system, a bank may issue a certificate in the market that would basically be called a derivative. This business is going on in Spain, just as it is in other markets. That certificate may be issued on the DAX100, the 100 largest equities on the German stock exchange; however, that does not mean that the bank actually invests in DAX100 equities. The underlying assets may actually be, for example, Japanese equities, in which case what the investor is buying is not actually what they think it is.

This is a dangerous exercise. Derivatives have been used extensively for refinancing because banks have been able to get money at much lower rates through certificates or derivatives than through other means, such as bonds or equities. Ultimately, this can lead, as in the Lehman Brothers case, to serious illiquidity. With mechanisms in place to ensure that the instruments that investors are putting their money into are actually backed by the assets that they suppose, the outcome could have been quite different. As it was, money was not channelled into the investments that the investors believed to be the case, creating huge risks, but was very much used to provide liquidity for ordinary banking operations.

Simply ensuring that companies are investing where they are supposed to would do a lot to counter the derivatives problem, and the transparency of Islamic finance offers some solution to this issue. When the investor selects a *Shari'a*-compliant instrument, he can be assured that his money is invested in equity and not in other, highly leveraged products, such as can be the case in conventional finance.

Another problem of the current system is that the bondholders are somehow immune from pain. As has been seen in the recent financial crisis, when corporations default, that debt is converted into sovereign debt. This then translates into the risk of potential sovereign defaults – for instance, in the cases of Greece and other countries. The debt burden simply gets shifted along the line. This was what happened in the 1996–97 South East Asian Crisis. At that time, the IMF moved in and imposed the condition of converting quasi-government and corporate debt into sovereign debt for repayment. The point is that the bondholders did not suffer. In the past, where bondholders have got burnt – for example, in the default of Argentina – that country has been singled out for exceptional punishment by investors.

It is now widely accepted that excessive leverage is risky, and this is echoed in Islamic finance. The only way to reduce this is to remove the default preference for debt. However, before tackling the tax treatment of bondholders, there are alternatives to be discussed, for example, contingent convertible bonds. These are a form of debt that will convert to equity, which means that the bondholders will also have to share the pain. This eliminates the 'too big to fail' scenario, since it will require lenders to examine more closely the quality of their lending, since they may also share in the losses. The present scenario is essentially taxpayer-guaranteed. The situation in Greece showed that, if it is a solvency problem, then throwing money at it is not a solution. Somehow, the bondholders must be required to take a haircut. In that case, they would have been German, French and British banks. However, an approach of this type would usher in a new system which is more equity-orientated, and that is where synergies exist between Islamic finance and Western finance.

Islamic finance does not claim to eliminate the possibility of crises occurring. Historically, there have been some crises. However, *Shari'a* law tries to establish instructions that will minimise their impact and avoid serious problems. The current financial crisis started from mortgages but spread to the real economic system. In Islamic finance, it is not possible to have debt out of debts, so a crisis that begins in the mortgage sector, for example, will not be transferred to other investments and other sectors of the economy.

The nature of contracts in Islamic finance, as is required by *Shari'a* law, is much simpler than is usually found in Western finance. For example, it is forbidden to combine two contracts. Additional complexity in contracts makes them less transparent, which can cause problems.

It was the misevaluation of assets that was a major cause of the crisis, be those physical assets, like real-estate, or financial assets. History gives many examples of crises that started from assets not being valued correctly by the market. How to avoid this problem has not been well explored to date; however, one solution could be to set supervisory measures for the valuation of assets and establish macro-prudential tools in corporations and enterprises. It is important from an institutional point of view that monetary authorities around the world set up these tools to avoid the future misevaluation of assets.

How genuine are Western financial institutions in applying Islamic financial contracts? Are they seeking the petro-dollar resources only?

One potentially controversial response to this question is to take the position that whatever their intentions are, they are their own to consider, and they have a right to them. Their intentions, for better or worse, do not detract from the good that comes from applying Islamic finance. What is important is what Muslim economists can offer to Western financial institutions and governments in solving the problems that their own economic models have brought about. Can Islamic finance introduce new modes of finance and re-balance contracts, and will that be successful in resolving the issues highlighted by the crisis?

During your time here in Madrid, you may have heard about the needs of Madrid with respect to financing public projects. If Islamic modes of finance can provide a better solution to achieve that, then why should they not be applied? This is the type of criterion by which Western financiers will evaluate the importance of Islamic finance. The standards of quality and purity from *riba*, *gharar* and *maysir* are the concern of the Islamic community.

If Western institutions are simply pursuing the petro-dollar resources only, then that is fine. The real challenge for those institutions is to create a situation where everyone will win through creating a truly Islamic mode of financing.

This question raises the issue of *niyya*, the intention, and Islam teaches that God alone knows the intention behind the acts of any individual, so this should not be the concern of anyone else. If someone is using Islamic modes of financing to raise resources for projects in his own country, there is no harm. If the conditions of doing that are more favourable than other, conventional alternatives, there should be no obstacle to doing that as long as it complies with *Shari'a* law. Delving into the question of *niyya* will not benefit anyone. All human beings try to increase their profits, and if an Islamic mode of finance benefits the investor with a use for his funds, and the borrower with more favourable conditions, then all is well and good.

Perhaps the wider adoption of Islamic finance in the West, regardless of the motivation, will have an impact on the moral standing of society, and perhaps it will not. What is important is that the transaction benefits both parties.

There are many innovations in Islamic finance. However, some of them are still disputed despite having been approved by leading *Shari'a* scholars. One of these innovative products is designed so that the investor places his money on the basis of a *Shari'a* contract. But, there is a swap of the returns with something else that is completely beyond the investor's control. This essentially allows the Muslim investor to use *Shari'a*-compliant methods to participate in an income stream which may be non-*Shari'a* compliant. This is because it is done with two contracts, possibly since using a single contract would make the non-*Shari'a*-compliant elements transparent to the investor, removing ignorance as a defence.

This type of instrument has been approved by *Shari'a* scholars. However, while it may not be so beneficial to dwell on the intentions of those using them, attention should be paid to the possibilities that may arise from using such contracts, for example, using Muslim investors' money to finance non-*Shari'a*-compliant activities, which would be a problem. Unfortunately, it is not possible to say that the existence of a *Shari'a* board is sufficient to prevent this, because *Shari'a* boards in this case are part of the problem, having sanctioned these profit rate swaps and other more advanced derivatives.

So, although the motivation of individuals in the transaction may not be the point, it does make sense to look at the immediate legal aspects of a transaction to consider how it might be deployed. It may be difficult to imagine how a *Shari'a* scholar could come to approve such a product; however, the documentation associated with these contracts as issued by Western investment banks is explicit in their intention to facilitate the participation of Muslim investors in non-*Shari'a*-compliant transactions. That is the basic concept, and prominent *Shari'a* scholars have approved it.

One useful comparison with respect to how innovative new products are accepted by the Islamic finance industry may be the ethical investment industry in the early 1990s. At that time, within the ethical investment sector, there were two camps. On one side, the 'dark green' were very strict, very purist, and would reject 80 to 90 per cent of the London Stock Exchange. The other group were known as the 'light green' and had the attitude that it was not possible to change the world overnight, so they would use more subtle pressure to direct things towards their goal. Perhaps it is not possible to achieve 100 per cent purity, or to have something that is completely 'impure', but it is more likely that it is a continuum along which each person will ultimately position themselves. Possibly the same could be said for *Shari'a* scholars; some will focus on control, while others would prefer more persuasive methods. The result should be an industry that is not so polarised but is more fluid in terms of what is deemed acceptable or unacceptable.

Part of the problem comes from the role of *Shari'a* committees in many Islamic banks. Contracts are presented to these groups of scholars, who consider the proposal, ultimately placing various conditions on the contract, and issue their approval of the contract and those conditions. What is really required, and it is something that has been called for for some time, is that some members of the *Shari'a* committee go to the market and see what the actual practice is; the forms being filled in by the customer, the extent of the contract and what the small print says. The *Shari'a* committee will give general guidelines and conditions; however, the actual practice is very important.

It is true that there are different schools of thought with respect to Islamic finance around the world – for example, between Malaysia and the Gulf states. Of course, they are based on the same core principles, the same important questions and issues, but there are differences. There are those who come with new interpretations, called *ijtihad* or *qiyas*, from which new products are derived. It is then discovered later that the resulting practice is not what was intended to be approved.

These differences of interpretation are highlighted by the comments made by Muhammad Taqi Usmani, Chairman of the International Shari'a Council for the Accounting and Auditing Organization for Islamic Financial Institutions (AAOIFI) in Bahrain. In a study of the *sukuk* industry, he discovered that 85 per cent of the instruments in the market are not *Shari'a* compliant, because the contracts do not coincide with the *fatwa*.

There have been cases of *Shari'a* advisors who have spoken out within *Shari'a* committees regarding the question of ensuring that funds are used in the proper manner. However, these same individuals have found that when their memberships on their committees were up for renewal, they were not endorsed. Essentially they were fired. The reality is that *Shari'a* board members have a vested interest in maintaining their memberships on their committees; thus there is pressure on those *Shari'a* advisors to accept certain things that are not really *Shari'a* compliant.

One possible solution to this problem could be to use *Shari'a* committees to serve a similar type of role for industry regulators, probably at a national level through the central bank or some other type of institution that would exact a fee for their services. This would be instead of the present situation, where each bank has its own *Shari'a* board, thus removing the conflict of interests that is created when the position of the *Shari'a* advisors is linked to the fortunes of the individual banks.

These centralised *Shari'a* boards should comprise *Shari'a* scholars, of course, but also legal experts, bankers and business people, so that they can make the correct decision that incorporates the perspectives of all the relevant stakeholders. This is important, since the *fatwa* coming from that centralised institution would have to be followed by the whole industry. The current situation, in which each bank has its own advisors and pursues its own interests, is not good for the Islamic banking industry itself.

Is Islamic finance at a 'tipping point'?

In this question, what is meant by 'tipping point' is the point at which Islamic finance has established itself in the wider industry. At present, the general acceptance of Islamic finance is limited to the Middle East and South East Asia, and perhaps some small parts of the European financial industry. It seems that Islamic finance really lacks the global scale necessary to be considered more than a niche industry outside those regions. Outstanding *sukuk* debt worldwide, for example, perhaps $100 billion, is less than one per cent of the global market. The potential for Islamic finance, however, is clear, since the size of the market today is less than one per cent, but Muslims represent one-fifth of the global population.

It would appear that there are a number of obstacles that need to be addressed for Islamic finance to increase its credibility so that it may capture a greater share of global financial markets. As in any sector of the financial industry, transparency is the key to creating trust and gaining acceptance, as are well-defined standards and regulations. Islamic finance, however, also must contend with the question of how *Shari'a* law is interpreted, harmonising practices not just between institutions but between different global regions as well. Once this has been achieved, Islamic finance needs to create innovative, purely Islamic products that demonstrate the clear advantages they can have over their conventional counterparts.

With respect to the regulatory aspects and governance, there has been some research originated by IE Business School, which performed a network analysis of *Shari'a* scholars and their engagements around the world. What this has shown is that there are trends which would appear to run contrary to normally accepted rules of good governance. For example, out of perhaps 250 scholars, just five of them control 35 per cent of all institutions. The situation where one scholar can sit on 80 different *Shari'a* boards in 15 countries would not seem to meet the quality of regulatory oversight required by the AAOIFI standards. It is even the case that no minutes exist for certain *Shari'a* boards, such that no records exist of dissenting scholars who would not adhere to accepted principles.

Many regulatory issues need to be addressed. A centralised *Shari'a* board with a standardised approach could be the best way to manage the governance of the Islamic finance industry, which would build trust and confidence, allowing the industry to grow much more quickly than is seen today. The concentration in the current system is more limiting to the growth of the industry than helpful in driving the industry forward.

One notable distinction of Islamic finance is that, although the vast majority of conventional finance is interest-based, in Islamic finance there are about five different modes of financing, each one inspiring a number of different contracts. This creates a great number of opportunities for investors to become involved in this sector through innovative products. For example, *sukuk* can fall into around 12 different types, divided into four or five different types of contract, for instance *musharaka*, *mudaraba*, *salam* or *istisna'a*. Thus, the future of Islamic finance offers many opportunities.

Where is Islamic finance headed?

The future of Islamic finance shows much potential but is conditional on achieving certain things. First of all is the rigorous observance of *Shari'a* regulation, or the problems that have emerged in *sukuk* compliance will spread throughout the sector. The second requirement is the establishment of centralised *Shari'a* committees, either nationally or on a regional basis, governing all Islamic financial institutions and investment banks.

A third condition for the success of Islamic finance is its widespread acceptance by Muslim states and government authorities. This problem is diminishing due to the success it has enjoyed to date; however, there is still work to be done to promote government participation in its regulation. Moreover, a greater understanding of Islamic finance principles by central banks worldwide is also required, and this is another necessity. It is unduly difficult for Islamic banks to comply with central banks' regulations intended for conventional financial institutions in Western countries. It would be preferable that the central banks of Islamic countries hold jurisdiction over Islamic banks. The tools are different, and the outcomes are different.

The final requirement is that Islamic finance gains a greater share of global financial markets. This is something that can be achieved through focusing on the preceding points. This is the discussion that needs to take place, and these are points that need to be worked on and researched.

The question of creating national *Shari'a* committees has been raised in the past, but that is immediately rejected by the governors of the central banks. This is because the central banks are not willing to accept another authority over themselves, which would necessarily be the case, since the *Shari'a* committee would be positioned to rule on the decisions of the central banks. Therefore, unless the central banks are themselves committed to making Islamic finance truly Islamic and are willing to accept the rulings of such a committee, the idea of centralised *Shari'a* boards is not practical.

It is to be expected that central banks will be resistant to the imposition of a higher Islamic authority; however, the issue remains that within a given region, country or even, occasionally, the same city, Islamic banks do not share the same opinions and apply the *Shari'a* standards in the same way. One step in the right direction would be for the commercial Islamic banks to come together to reach an agreement, a concordance, amongst themselves. Establishing this type of industry body with independent judgement and views would be a strong demonstration from those banks of their willingness to have an independent third party judging their compliance. Starting with commercial Islamic banks is the first stage, before tackling the central banks.

The creation of centralised *Shari'a* committees may, however, bring about some disadvantages, and for this reason there are those who favour industry self-regulation. The potential problems may not be so different to the current situation. Whereas today the issue is that Islamic scholars may sit on more *Shari'a* boards than is optimal, the commitments of those scholars may also be excessive if one committee is made responsible for the large number of Islamic financial institutions that might exist in a country.

Self-regulation and time for those regulations to evolve are preferable to having a handful of individuals defining the sector. Placing the authority with such a limited group of scholars will discourage creativity in the industry. The history of *fiqh* and *Shari'a* shows that there are different schools of thought. Everyone, with whatever perspective, may contribute their views to the evolution of the regulations; however, *Shari'a* committees restrict that privilege to those members of the committee, who ultimately impose their own view.

This is a very relevant question because there is an intense debate going on in Islamic finance circles around the issue of *Shari'a*-compliant finance and banking and *Shari'a*-based finance and banking. This issue is very much in the domain of the Islamic commercial banks. In the discussion of Islamic economics and finance, it is important not to neglect the economics aspect; however, this seems to be a strong point of divergence between the value-driven aspirations of Islamic economics and the practical reality of Islamic finance.

Islamic finance and economics was originally conceived as a response to poverty and lack of development and remains at the heart of the initiative. However, what has been adopted in the industry is an entirely commercial model of Islamic banking. Unfortunately, this system has worked to mimic conventional financial products and does not impact in the positive manner initially intended. Thus, the significant problem that Islamic economics ought to be addressing remains that of human-centred development and poverty. This is not the case only in poor countries – even Saudi Arabia has problems of poverty.

Addressing this poverty dilemma requires a new approach to achieving the original objectives. It is probably not possible to reinvent the commercial Islamic banks given the way that they are, so a new institutionalisation is called for. The 1960s saw the origins of Islamic banking as social banking in Egypt and in Malaysia. In the 1970s, commercial Islamic banking emerged, and it is working today. The correlation between financial development and economic growth must be acknowledged. However, there are still those who are excluded from the financial system, even under Islamic finance. There is a social failure there which has lead to an increase in consumption as a result of Islamic banking, which was not the intention.

A revival of the original intentions of Islamic economics through a new option, a third stage of Islamic banking institutionalisation, to operate in addition to commercial Islamic banking, to be able to respond to the core issues of economic development, is required. The structure of that institutionalisation is not obvious. However, the European Union researched social banking; therefore, there must be some experience that can be drawn upon.

It may appear confusing to be discussing, on the one hand, the reconciliation of Islamic finance with traditional Western finance and how that can be achieved by using asset-backed contracts, then, on the other hand, insisting upon strict commitment to *Shari'a* regulation. The reality is that the goal must be to follow *Shari'a* principles completely, and this cannot be sacrificed. It is possible to observe the circumstances and adjust the structure accordingly, but the optimal solution, even considering any modification, must be fully *Shari'a* compliant.

The role of Islamic banking with respect to addressing poverty should not be misunderstood. Islamic banks are not charitable organisations, and their existence alone will not eliminate poverty. The Islamic concept of charity is known as *zakah* and has been mentioned; however, another very important concept is *al-waqf*, the trust or endowment. In the United States, you can visit many universities and find that there are buildings worth millions of dollars that have been endowed to the university by alumni and other benefactors. This is *waqf*; however, the Americans making those donations probably have no Islamic connection, just an interest in contributing to the growth of their country. The solution to the problems of poverty and development will not result from the use of just one tool, but from the whole package, including reducing conspicuous consumption.

It is not expected that Islamic banks should be charitable by definition, but it is important that there be something that distinguishes them from conventional banks, that differentiates those institutions bearing the name 'Islamic'. The definition was coined in the 1970s and laid out certain goals and objectives, such as economic development, for which there is still a great need. Institutions with the title 'Islamic' need to be responsible for that and the moral package that entails, but it is important to recognise that that moral package is not just in the form of *Shari'a* compliance and the *fiqh* process. It can be seen that even when compliance is achieved, and products are *halal*, there is still a social failure. That failure will not be solved with current commercial Islamic banking; hence, a new institutionalisation is essential to address those issues.

How is CAMEL (capital adequacy, asset quality, management, earnings and liquidity) different for Islamic banking versus conventional banking?

The CAMEL criteria, used to measure the efficiency of banks, are designed for conventional banks. Islamic banks are, of course, quite different and cannot be compared with the same measurements.

With respect to capital adequacy, the Basel Accords require that this is some eight per cent of the assets held by the bank, weighted by risk. This is to ensure that the bank is able to cover the risk liability of the deposits it holds. For Islamic banks, this is not necessary, since Muslim customers must be prepared to share the risks of the bank, since this is inherent in the principles of Islamic finance. Whatever the products used, whether they be *mudaraba*, *musharaka* or others, the capital of the bank must be *fiqh*-observant. So, capital adequacy should be viewed differently because it is not necessary to protect the investment deposits of the bank, but rather the assets must bear the risk associated with using those assets in profit-sharing modes of finance and should not be protected.

Asset quality, of course, is also different in Islamic finance, since it uses equity-based investments. This is also an intrinsic aspect of Islamic finance: to participate in the risk on the asset and the liability side. Therefore, the assets themselves are different, being more diverse and higher in risk than for conventional investment banks.

The question could be asked as to why Islamic banks should not work to minimise their exposure to risk, selecting lower-risk assets, since they are dealing with their customers' money. Of course, the risk can be minimised, but it is the nature of the assets that they are risk-loaded. A portfolio of equity-based assets is preferred over sale-based modes of financing because of the additional added value that it generates, similar to conventional banks, which implies riskier assets.

Management quality in Islamic finance is highly important, particularly because the assets in which the banks are dealing are more risky. The Islamic finance institutions should have more experience dealing with risk, pricing it correctly and passing on that price and the returns to the customers.

Earnings for Islamic banks should be comparable with those of other institutions and compatible with the class of assets under consideration. Assets with greater risk should return higher earnings.

There are two considerations for the liquidity position of Islamic banks. For the investment deposits, liquidity does not represent a problem, since the fund will be tied up in projects, and the investor will have to wait to recover their deposit. For demand deposits, however, the bank requires the liquidity to cover those deposits. This could be achieved using *musharaka*, the participation mode of financing, with the development of a secondary market for selling those participatory interests. On average, however, assets will be less liquid than in conventional finance, since it is prohibited to sell debt contracts, and banks cannot borrow money if there is a short-term need for liquidity.

Finally, sensitivity plays a major role in Islamic banks because they are dealing with risk, more so than conventional banking, so careful risk analyses should be performed to monitor their level of risk exposure.

These are the major differences that should be accounted for in developing criteria for measuring the efficiency of Islamic banks using the CAMEL model, and they should be taken into account.

These questions have raised a number of very important issues, and they require greater attention from Islamic economists and financiers. One of those is *Shari'a* boards and their role in Islamic financial institutions. Should they be responsible simply for ensuring financial instruments' *Shari'a* compliance, or should they also concern themselves with the social responsibility aspects of the banks' investments? At present, the social responsibility aspect seems to be neglected. Much effort is expended debating the *Shari'a* compliance of the various products, but the contributions of those investments to the humanitarian goals of Islamic economics, like the removal of poverty and the reduction of conspicuous consumption in Muslim societies, are largely overlooked. Both aspects need to be kept under consideration: that the products offered are *halal* and that they fulfil the objectives of social development.

Probably, under the current scenario, an Islamic bank would be willing to finance the importation of luxury cars in a poor country like Pakistan, Egypt or Indonesia before considering the implications for improving the conditions for the wider community. The importation of expensive luxury cars from Germany to Muslim countries, under the considerations of CAMEL, represents a very good class of asset, but may not contribute well to the realisation of social objectives like creating employment, reducing poverty, reducing the balance of payments deficit and reducing the budgetary deficit of the government. Many such concerns are ignored when *Shari'a* boards restrict themselves to the limited objectives of maintaining *Shari'a* compliance while maximising profits for the banks.

With respect to earnings, the financial industry is very competitive, and it is not realistic to expect banks not to concern themselves with their profitability. Minor differences may be tolerable, but the shareholders in a bank are unlikely to accept returns of just five per cent while other banks are earning ten per cent. It is often stated that this would be acceptable, especially to Muslim and socially responsible investors, but the question is far from settled, and the Islamic banks also have an obligation to satisfy their shareholders.

This is compounded by the liquidity problems faced by Islamic institutions. Being unable to raise funds quickly on the basis of interest, as conventional banks can do in almost any sector of the economy, Islamic banks are required to hold higher level of liquidity. It may be possible to create an institution to facilitate the raising of short-term liquidity in a *Shari'a*-compliant manner that would help Islamic banks in this regard, but it is something that has not yet been realised, and therefore the problem remains. As a result, it is occasionally necessary for the banks to use conventional methods, which draws criticism, which may or may not be justified. If the need for liquidity is there, and it is not possible to raise the required funds Islamically, then the banks face being unable to honour their commitments and thus their own failure. These problems are sometimes overlooked when passing judgement on Islamic institutions.

Extended discussions have been held amongst leading scholars at the best schools of business and economics around the world over whether scholars in Islamic banks should concern themselves only with ensuring their products are *halal* or whether they should broaden their criteria to include societal and humanitarian considerations. These are important questions that have not yet been resolved. The objectives of maximising profits and social development are often in conflict with each other.

Islamic banks are commercial institutions with an obligation to deliver the expected profits to their shareholders. They must remain competitive in the market, yet they have the additional burden of upholding certain moral commitments. The criticism levelled at Islamic institutions for the compromises necessary to reconcile these objectives often places on them unrealistic demands to operate in the ideal manner, under which many of them would face failure.

3
Public–Private Partnerships: Islamic Finance in International Project Finance

Symposium workshop

IE Business School, Madrid, Spain, 17th June 2010

Chairmen

Ignacio de la Torre, Academic Director of Finance Programmes, IE Business School, Spain

Dr Mohamed A. Elgari, Former Director, Islamic Economics and Research Centre, King Abdulaziz University, Saudi Arabia

Special comments made by

Oliver Agha, Managing Partner, Agha & Shamsi, United Arab Emirates

The purpose of this discussion is to link Islamic finance to something concrete, something which is ultimately about real assets. Two areas in which Spain excels are infrastructure projects and renewable energy installations. Both of these represent very good asset classes for Islamic finance; hence the decision to hold a session to lay out some of the practical solutions for structured finance of these projects in a manner that is *Shari'a* compliant.

Taking into account the risks unique to infrastructure finance, which Islamic financial products best fit infrastructure projects?

Infrastructure projects are themselves unique. They are expensive 'mega-projects' that have a lot of risks, which makes private financiers hesitant to commit to projects that may take years to complete. The risks are not limited to credit and financial risk but may also include technology risk, sovereign risk, even political risk. The question is how all of these risks are addressed within an Islamic framework.

Project finance transactions, from a conventional and from an Islamic perspective, are quite different to corporate finance transactions. In addition to their scale and risk allocation, they are typically 'off-balance sheet' transactions by definition, with limited or no recourse on the investor side. This should be borne in mind as the fundamental difference between the two.

With respect to the instruments, it is helpful to distinguish the types of projects available and map the different types of Islamic instruments available to the types of projects. One example is the public–private partnership, where there is a concession; that is to say, the asset or project is existing, and the distinguishing feature of the project is that it is not 'green-field'. This is typically financed with a hybrid, 'conventional plus Islamic' structure, where equity would be contributed by Muslim investors, or *Shari'a*-inclined investors, while the debt would be in the form of a conventional bank loan. Those would be the two sources of capital.

A lease contract is then used, between the project company, which would hold the equity, and a funding company, which would hold the debt and, usually, ownership of the project assets. The funding company then enters into an *ijarah*, or 'lease back' agreement.

Another example is that of the financing of a new bridge across the Bosphorus undertaken by the current Prime Minister of Turkey while he was the Mayor of Istanbul. In order to do so without interest, it was sold as 'BOT Participation Financing', essentially using a BOT (Build-Operate-Transfer) model based on *musharaka*. The first step was the *musharaka*, the public partnership. However, the contractors wanted to receive payment before the project was completed, so the second step was the application of what in *Shari'a* is called *ijarah mausufah fi aldhimmah*, or a described or forward lease, where an asset under construction is considered to be owned by the contractor and is leased to the purchaser before it is delivered. This model has been applied very successfully in Saudi Arabia and the Gulf countries, as well as in South East Asia.

With respect to projects that are jointly financed, the equity part Islamically and the rest conventionally, there are regulations in Islamic finance which prohibit investment in companies or projects that have a debt-to-equity ratio greater than 1:3, which poses a potential obstacle, since large infrastructure projects tend to be characterised by leverage of 3:1. It can be seen today that Islamic markets have the capacity to fund projects up to a total of $5 billion, so there is the ability within the Islamic institutions, with Western partners, to execute 100 per cent Islamic financing.

There is a very good example in the PLUS Expressways Berhad, concession holder and operator of 62 per cent of toll motorways in peninsular Malaysia. They are raising capital and equity on a *Shari'a* basis, using five or six different financing tools. It is important to note also that if the project is financed 100 per cent Islamically, then those leverage restrictions do not apply.

Alternatively, there is a concept in *Shari'a* called *wakalah*, which allows for the appointment of an agent to perform a transaction on the behalf of another in return for a fee. The use of such an agent to make an investment creates a kind of hybridisation, something between equity and debt, which can be used to manage some of those issues. This is important under a civil law jurisdiction, for example, Spain, where the use of the term *musharaka* would oblige the parties to become partners. Common law countries, like the UK and the US, make *Shari'a* financing much easier, due to the ability to separate title ownership from beneficial ownership, or usufruct. The beneficial ownership is not fictitious; it is a real ownership, however, the ownership is not of the asset, but of the proceeds from the exploitation of that asset.

Bangladesh is an example of a country that can benefit greatly from this kind of financing. The country has a great need of infra structure; however, the government is unable to fund these projects. The normal recourse is to go to the International Monetary Fund (IMF); however, given the requirements, the government devised an infrastructure fund, inviting private investors to enter into that fund through a *musharaka* structure. The reason for doing this kind of project financing is that individuals and governments cannot undertake projects of this scale alone, so an infusion of capital is achieved through a public–private partnership. It is clear how this is achieved using conventional project financing, but the issue at hand is how can this be achieved Islamically.

One way is the structure described, using *ijarah* and forward lease and such things. However, *sukuk* can also be brought into this context, even for 'green-field' projects. It is a way of tapping into the funds in the hands of smaller investors. Even in Bangladesh, there is a lot of liquidity in savings, but the smaller investors want some sort of protection for the capital they are contributing.

So, this is an interesting challenge for *Shari'a* scholars: how to tap into that savings liquidity that exists, even in poor Islamic countries, and attract those funds for use in large infrastructure projects.

Often, the *rab ul-mal*, the investor, is reluctant to enter into a *mudaraba* contract without some form of guarantee, but in this type of contract the *mudarib*, the project manager, cannot give that guarantee. However, the government, as a third party, and in order to promote the greater public interest, or *maslaha*, can guarantee those *mudaraba* bonds. These *mudaraba* bonds can be sold easily because of the huge captive market of Muslim investors who are seeking *Shari'a*-compliant investments with the protection of a guarantee.

Typically, with infrastructure projects, there is some kind of agreement in place that offers some guarantee of cash flow; for instance, toll road projects include a guarantee of minimum tolls revenue, particularly since forecasts are generally found to be overly optimistic. For power-generation projects, there would be a 'power purchase agreement' guaranteeing that the utility distributor will purchase at least a minimum amount of electricity, at a certain rate, over the lifetime of the plant, which may be 20 years. Such guarantees are very much part of Islamic finance and can be issued from the government directly, or they may sponsor another party to do it.

A few years ago, a *fatwa* was issued by the Fiqh Academy of the Organisation of the Islamic Conference (OIC) concerning *sukuk al mudaraba*, but unfortunately it was never implemented. It specifically states that any third party, especially the government, may offer this kind of guarantee. The Accounting and Auditing Organisation for Islamic Financial Institutions (AAOIFI) has also outlined in detail in its standards the manner in which projects can be guaranteed. The problem is that, unfortunately, no private party is willing to offer this guarantee for free, and governments are not interested in guaranteeing the principle of project investors, except maybe in the case of specific infrastructure projects.

These are not the only options available. Once the public–private partnership has been agreed, the contracts can be designed in whatever manner is appropriate to the project; for instance, as a profit-generating venture or a non-profit infrastructure project. *Musharaka, istisna'a, mudaraba* and *ijarah* are all possible.

The Islamic Development Bank (IDB) has been active in trying to overcome these issues, not only financing infrastructure projects, but also acting as guarantor in such financing modes. For the future of Islamic finance in Europe, an institution that has an interest in this type of project, providing guarantees and support, like a development bank, would play a vital role. Such guarantees, of course, have a cost for governments and the institutions providing them. But if an infrastructure project is successful, it will bring public benefit and also generate tax revenues. It is thus possible that the cost of the guarantee could even be recouped from that tax revenue.

The historical city of Jeddah, the second largest in Saudi Arabia and home to around four million Saudis, has seen growing infrastructure problems over the years. One issue that has been raised lately is that of financing. The arguments have been that government finance is not sufficient or that the funds were not filtering through to the actual contractors, amongst others. It would seem that this is an opportunity for Islamic finance. An informal poll run recently via one website revealed that, amongst the residents of Jeddah, many would be prepared to pay municipal taxes to make Jeddah a better place to live. The investment will is there, but it is something that will not happen automatically. What is required is for someone to structure the project and market it.

It is important to note that it is possible to structure an infrastructure project financing Islamically at the same level of risk as conventional project financing, which is very important. The basic structure has been defined and implemented many times in many places. Islamic investors have their own legal entity, and the conventional investors have another. The Muslim investor, *al-mustasni'*, the buyer, can then enter into a procurement contract with the constructor of the project being financed, *al-sani'*, the seller. As the investors will own the assets once they have been completed, they can establish a forward lease of the assets to the proposer of the project owner, who will begin making payments, thus establishing a cash flow for investors from day one. The conventional investors can lend money directly to the project proposer. In this situation, there is no problem with the leverage being in excess of 1:3, since the Islamic investors are not holding equity in the project but rather own the assets under construction.

What is preventing non-Islamic countries from tackling *Shari'a*-based liquidity pools by issuing Islamic instruments to finance infrastructure projects?

In the case of Spain, as for many other countries, the main barrier to embracing Islamic finance is simply ignorance. Although those sources of liquidity in the Islamic sphere are very interesting, the instruments are not familiar to many Western financiers. Moreover, conventional project finance is dominated by concerns over leverage, and the infrastructure developers want to carry as little equity as possible. Ownership is also important because the development companies are evaluated on EBITDA and assured cash flows. It is one thing to discuss how projects can be structured in a manner that is complaint with *Shari'a*, but the competitiveness of those contracts compared to conventional project financing cannot be overlooked in the context of Western markets.

When Western companies, from Europe, the US and even Asia, enter the Islamic space, they are swift to learn and embrace Islamic tools for the purpose of doing business in Saudi Arabia, Malaysia or Indonesia. However, with the exception of the UK, there are a lot of difficulties with governments when trying to use Islamic finance in Europe. France opened the dialogue regarding Islamic finance some eight or nine years ago but has only done something concrete in the last two years or so. Will Spain and other countries take as long to implement something? There are certain changes necessary in the laws and regulations regarding financial transactions in order to allow Islamic finance to operate in Western markets. Those rules are particularly difficult to change in civil law countries, so government participation is necessary to create the flexibility to attract Islamic capital to join in European projects. There seems to be no problem for Western companies to enter into the Islamic sphere, but going in the other direction is difficult.

It is easy to be pessimistic about the speed at which politicians are able to tackle those kinds of reforms, but on the other hand, life has changed during this crisis. GE is issuing debt at a lower rate than the US government, and Telefónica is issuing debt at a lower risk than the Spanish government. Perhaps, then, it is possible to sidestep the politicians, and if Telefónica, for example, is interested in issuing *sukuk*, it can do so through a London-based SPV under English law and have it listed in London. It may not be necessary that European governments tackle tax reforms if global corporations can find other ways to perform these transactions.

However, this scenario is unlikely to serve the required purpose in the case of, for instance, a Spanish logistics company operating concessions in Spain and requiring euros deployed in Spain. For collateral purposes and the protection of investor's rights, it may be necessary that the entity invest in Spain directly, in which case the support of government is required.

Taxation issues are certainly one area where reforms would be necessary to put Islamic finance on a level playing field with conventional finance, however, another is concession agreements and their transferability. A concession is an agreement between the government and a specific party, so the question is whether a third party can invest in that concession without violating the terms of that agreement. Government also has an important role to play in the aforementioned guarantees for investors and the risk management of the resultant cash flow of a project.

It is important that those issues that represent an obstacle to the greater use of Islamic finance in the Western society are identified. Once those barriers have been identified then steps can be taken, by governments and the financial industry, to begin to address some of them, as has been done in the UK and in France, and realise the advantages of Islamic finance as a real and competitive alternative.

European involvement in Islamic finance can be thought of in several forms. One is in terms of savings being invested in European countries, like Spain, but there is also the situation of European companies becoming involved in Islamically financed projects in the Middle East, where they will be under the jurisdiction of local laws in those countries. Even if it is difficult to do adopt *Shari'a*-compliant financing in Spain, Spanish companies are now apparently getting involved in many concessions and Islamically financed contracts in the Middle East.

Projects may be arranged through a subsidiary, or other entity, in the Middle East, but if the physical asset and the payments are located or originate in Spain, for example, then they will be subject to the Spanish taxation regime. Therefore, the project is exposed to double taxation, taxes being payable on each transfer of the ownership of the asset. This is a burden that the project managers cannot afford, so the location of the asset can have a large impact on the result. However, this issue has been addressed in certain countries, such as the United Kingdom, and the law has been changed in some other countries as well.

The prevailing law in any jurisdiction is an important consideration when adopting Islamic financial products. A *fatwa* may be issued endorsing a particular transaction, according to Islamic law, in a non-Muslim country, but that *Shari'a* ruling might not be recognised or respected under the law of that country. The point is that with many Western markets becoming increasingly interested in Islamic finance, it is important to create the legal and regulatory infrastructure to support those instruments, so that Muslim investors can have the confidence to put their money in these foreign-based projects. This is one of the hidden legal risks that are not often discussed.

This is related to the earlier point regarding civil law and common law countries. There has been very little experience of Islamic finance in civil law countries, since most of the work in the West so far has been in common law countries. In common law countries, the focus is much more on enforcement of the contract itself, so if all of the books of *fiqh* are included in the contract, they will be enforced. What would happen in a civil law environment is largely unknown, but that is not to say that it is a closed door. Where there is a will there is a way, so it is necessary to start implementing Islamic finance in civil law countries and see what will surface, in the sincere hope that it will not be necessary for any case to go to court.

If construction companies and infrastructure developers in Spain and the rest of Europe, can agree on a common position and send a clear message to the government, then the government might react. What is important there is that agreement and that what is put forward is a common proposal. One of the advantages of secular countries is that their laws are not derived from the word of God, so they can be changed at any time.

With respect to competition, GE issued *sukuk* valued at $500 million in 2009, and it was not cheap for them. They paid a higher price than if they had issued the debt conventionally, which raises the question of what their motivation was for doing so. They might have considered that this higher, regional price was worthwhile in order to tackle this new source of liquidity, or it may have been more of a public relations exercise. As with any *sukuk*, it may not be exactly clear what is hidden until it reaches maturity. However, it is an important consideration, since any Western companies considering issuing this kind of instrument will first consider the question of cost, and there must be a strong argument for using an alternative instrument if they are more expensive than conventional debt.

There was the case of a Swedish asset management company that issued *sukuk* worth €300 million, comparable to the GE *sukuk*, based in Germany. The motivation for it is in looking to tap into the liquidity of the Middle Eastern countries. The main additional costs in that issuance were basically due to the lack of experience in the procedure for gaining *Shari'a* approvals and issuing *sukuk*. The legal aspects and different governance issues will cost a little more, but not significantly so. Where this particular *sukuk* manages the total cost is on the return. Middle Eastern investors have certain expectations about the return on their investments, which need to be considered carefully on a case-by-case basis.

Are Islamic and non-Islamic finance compatible?

The origin of any kind of financing, Islamic or conventional, is the same. That is the need of funds in order to do something, be that buying a house, buying a car or financing a project. From that perspective, Islamic finance is just another way of achieving the same thing. One definition of 'compatible', therefore, could be that one is a perfect substitute for the other.

A more interesting definition in this context is 'living together harmoniously', in which case many would say that conventional finance and Islamic finance are compatible, as has been evidenced by a number of large, quasi-infrastructure projects, such as Rabigh–Yansab a large petrochemical project in Saudi Arabia, where there was an Islamic tranche of $836 million and a conventional tranche of $4.5 billion side-by-side, with very intricate inter-creditor relationships orchestrated between the two parties.

Going into the deeper, spiritual question of the compatibility of Islamic and conventional finance, one must look to the Abrahamic religious roots of the prohibition of usury. This is something that conventional finance has abandoned. So, from that spiritual perspective it would seem that they can never be truly compatible. However, on a practical level there is congruence, and it is possible to create a structure of something where the Islamic financiers own a piece of the project assets, which get leased to the non-Muslim project company, and Islamic and conventional finance exist alongside each other.

This response, however, is to address the question from a secular, Western point of view – a technical, non-Islamic perspective. The charging of interest is completely incompatible with Islamic finance; thus, for a Muslim, the use of conventional finance is not an option.

Taking the notion of compatibility as two alternatives being perfect mutual substitutes, when designing a fund or a financing structure of a hybrid nature it can be helpful to use an approach that may be referred to as the 'Principle of Indifference'. That would mean designing the finance in such a way that all stakeholders, for instance, financiers and contractors are indifferent to participating in the project under the hybrid structure or under a homogeneous structure such as would be typical in their own jurisdiction, be that conventional or Islamic.

From an operational perspective, this usually means that there would be a special purpose vehicle (SPV), which is the link between the funding company and the developer. The result is that, in the US, for example, contractors on residential contracts can use the standard architectural contracts and industry standards, so there are no additional transaction costs incurred, and the *Shari'a* investors are satisfied because there is a separation. So, in the end, they are compatible and indifferent.

Examples of this type of financing structure, which has been used multiple times since 1988, include the Hub River project in Pakistan, Equate in Kuwait and, recently, the Amman Airport in Jordan. A particular set of assets are ring-fenced and acquired by the Islamic financiers, which are then leased to the project, whether it be an operating lease or a lease that ends in ownership, and the conventional financiers lend money to the project under a different contract.

With respect to accounting, it is relatively simple. If there is a *sukuk* or infrastructure financing with the possibility to have half financed conventionally and the other half Islamically, it is not difficult to separate the two. The Islamic accounting rules and regulations are very detailed, very clear and based on International Financial Reporting Standards. So, from the accounting perspective, which is of very important for Islamic structuring, there is not an issue with compatibility.

One part of the question is the compatibility of finance having an Islamic tranche and a non-Islamic tranche together. There are many examples. The deeper question lies in the main principles of Islamic finance; prohibition of *riba*, *gharar* and *maysir*, profit- and loss-sharing, and *maslaha*. There is a commonality between those things and the Judeo-Christian tradition, but there has been a break between that tradition and the *maqasid*, the objectives and purpose of Islamic law, that grandiose design that is envisioned by Islamic finance. The name is not as important as the objective of bringing the greater good to all of humanity.

The phenomenon of *riba*, for example, is not acceptable to a Muslim, not simply because it is contrary to the teachings of the *Qur'an*, but because of its effect on society. There are research studies that have shown that interest is actually the cause of instability in the world's financial markets. There is also the issue of money creation, where cash deposits are being used to generate five times that amount of credit. If there is some common ground where Muslim and Western economists can work together, the issue of *riba* is one that must be solved. Looking at it from a non-denominational point-of-view, there can be no compromise on that, lest the problem which haunts conventional finance today also begin to affect Islamic finance.

It can be seen that when there is a project that is being financed both conventionally and Islamically, they would appear to be compatible and share most of the risks, but when it comes to the land, the plant or the assets of the project, there appears to be a prevalence of Islamic tranche, and the conventional financiers have a lower position. This is often perceived by Western financiers as being a sign of a certain inequality in these arrangements that should be addressed. Unfortunately, that would seem to be asking too much. A conventional lender places an obligation on the borrower, the project company, to pay back the debt, in the form of a mortgage on certain assets and sometimes through corporate guarantees. The Islamic investor, on the other hand, in place of that guarantee, that repayment obligation, takes ownership of the assets, which incorporates ownership risk. One must choose which side one prefers to be on – to have a guarantee of being repaid and secured assets, or to have ownership rights over the assets.

The spiritual aspect is a very important and integral part of Islamic project finance. It is so inherent that once one acknowledges that, everything seems a lot more sensible in the context of how projects are financed Islamically. A scholar once said, 'The collapse of society invariably results from two ideas: the first, "So long as I am full it matters not to me if others suffer", and the second, "You suffer hardship so that I may live at ease, you work so that I may eat".'

These ideas are not unique to Islam. They are clearly enunciated in the Old Testament, Ezekiel 22:12, where usurers are cast in a particularly negative light. Jesus Christ was also quite specific when he spoke to this, saying, 'Love your enemies and do not lend again.' Other notable scholars throughout history, including Moses, Aristotle, Thomas Aquinas, John Maynard Keynes and Adam Smith have all cautioned against usury and in some instances clearly condemned it. It would appear that often there is a perception that Islam is unique in its prohibition of usury, however this is not the case. It is universal, acclaimed by all religions. There are even ancient Hindu and Buddhist doctrines that speak of how usury eventually brings societies down.

From this spiritual foundation, it can be seen that Islamic project financing is simply based in this notion of just and equitable dealing with all parties. There is a *hadith* which says that in any circumstances where justness does not prevail, that contract has lost its fundamental spiritual basis.

Project finance, with its long time frames and diverse stakeholders, from project sponsors, to lenders, to government entities, is the sort of arrangement that is very well suited to Islamic financing, as has been seen over and over again. This has to do with the synergistic relationships and co-owner partnerships. In a conventional project financing the project company has an obligation to repay the lenders, secured against the assets. If that obligation is not met, in conventional non-recourse financing, the financiers will have 'step in' rights, or novation rights, which means that they will take over the role of the project company and operate the assets in order to recoup their investment. In that sense, the risk being borne by the investors in conventional project finance is remarkably similar to the risk of Islamic investors, making project financing perhaps the one area of conventional finance that is closest to its Islamic counterpart in terms of forming partnerships and working together.

In Islamic project financing there is, invariably, an SPV established, which is financed with funds from Islamic financiers. These investors then take the project assets, or a portion of them, and lease those to the project company. The notable difference is that this is not the lending of money with an absolute obligation to repay but is actually investing in the assets of the project, taking ownership of assets and leasing them to the project company.

There have been projects, some worth up to $8.5 billion, where the multilateral lenders have been very interested in coming as close as possible to the conventional risk profile they were used to, and it is possible to get quite close. The difference between Islamic finance and conventional finance is like the difference between grape juice and wine; it cannot be exactly the same, because if it is, you have now turned the grape juice into wine, and it has become *haram*, impermissible. The art of calibrating the structure so that it remains 'grape juice' is an art and is also a very important discipline for our esteemed scholars and those that work with them.

So, put simply, Islamic project finance is a carefully orchestrated arrangement where the Islamic financiers end up owning a portion of the assets and then leasing them to the project company, and there are many different options concerning payments and transfer and ownership between the parties. The bottom line is that, in the end, the ownership of the assets is transferred back to the project company, and the lease payments constitute the return on the financiers' investment.

The same concept would apply with infrastructure projects involving the government. One such project involving the Saudi government involved granting a concession to a project company that then used that structure to build, to own and to effectively operate the resulting assets until they had recouped their costs and envisioned profits. Once that had been achieved, the usufruct reverted to government ownership, and thus an equitable agreement was reached that was acceptable to both parties.

The golden rule in Islam, and Islamic finance, is that whatever is not expressly prohibited is permissible. There are a few things that are strictly impermissible, and there are no ways around them. There is no way to make usury permissible. It is not possible to make Islamic champagne. There is a huge amount that is permissible, except for those discrete aspects that are prohibited.

One landmark deal in Islamic finance was the Al-Waha deal, a $526 million polypropylene petrochemical plant in Al-Jubail City, Saudi Arabia, which was named 'Middle East Islamic Deal of the Year 2006' by *Project Finance Magazine* and 'Project Finance of the Year' by *Islamic Finance News*. It was the first deal ever done on a completely Islamic basis with diminishing *musharaka*. Today, a number of large Islamic entities are using a similar construct for their *ijarah*-based financing, so it has become a market leader in many respects. It employs an *ijarah*-based structure and a forward lease arrangement, where the financier starts to receive payments before the construction is completed, so the cash flow to investors is generated through advanced rent payments. Additionally, a service agency agreement is established, which goes some way to reassure the investors over their assuming the ownership risk associated with this structure and also passes some of those critical ownership risk elements back to the project company, however importantly, in a *Shari'a*-compliant manner. The legal documentation involved in such transactions is quite complex and voluminous, but standard approaches are evolving in the market, and there are *Shari'a* scholars who are increasingly comfortable with these arrangements.

There are those who would say that the defaults that have been witnessed in certain Islamic instruments suggest that Islamic finance is also being affected by the credit crunch. Defaults in any system would be reflective of that, but it is important, when examining those instruments, to consider whether the default is in an inherent *Shari'a* risk or whether it is a construct that has been included in order to replicate the conventional risk profile of such a product. An element of a default could come from something that does not really fit in with the *ijma'*, or the consensus of how that Islamic structure really should be. It could then be argued that the default in that case is not a truly Islamic default, since it is difficult to quantify a default within what should be a partnership. If there is a payment default, unless it is as a result of negligence on the part of the entity, it is very difficult to quantify from a *Shari'a* perspective. By that argument, the number of truly Islamic defaults would be very few; they would be serious, but then the risk would fall where it ought to fall.

Cross-Border Projects: Will the *Shari'a* board in country X have the same views/interpretations as the board in country Y with respect to key *Shari'a* issues?

With respect to Islamic finance, one often-made distinction is that between the 'Gulf model' and the 'Malaysian model', and in such discussions the differences are often exaggerated. They are not as great as some would portray them, and indeed there are signs that the two schools of thought are merging because of the effort of standardisation being undertaken by various institutions. AAOIFI is one such institution, and the recently established International Shari'a Research Academy for Islamic Finance (ISRA) in Malaysia has on its board *Shari'a* scholars from all over the world, which also helps in bringing together the disparate views, comparing notes and understanding each other. Fortunately, it can be seen that Malaysia is coming closer to the Gulf model, and people in the Gulf better understand the practices in Malaysia. However, there is still work to be done.

The main question is whether this is creating a problem for Islamic finance and banking, creating segmentation in the market which affects the fair pricing of instruments. What is important is not which policy is more advantageous in terms of pricing, but that standardisation removes any such segmentation, expanding the supply and demand and energising the market in order to achieve a fair equilibrium pricing.

One particular point of departure between these two schools of thought is the issue of *bai'al 'inah*, sale and repurchase, which involves two contracts where an asset is sold in one transaction for a lump sum, then resold for a higher price, possibly on credit in the other. It is a very popular instrument in Malaysia as a form of liquidity management and in the creation of money markets. However, it is not accepted as *Shari'a* compliant and is forbidden throughout the Cooperation Council for the Arab States of the Gulf (GCC). In Malaysia, this instrument has been challenged in court and has even been upheld as valid by the Malaysian Supreme Court, even though the National Shari'a Advisory Council has looked at the instrument and ruled that its use should be discouraged.

The Supreme Court of Malaysia ought not to be considered an authority on the *Shari'a* aspects of banking, since they have even admitted that lending with interest is permissible. What is important is that in Malaysia, more and more institutions are moving away from *'inah* and that a Saudi bank, Al Rajhi, has opened offices in Malaysia and is doing well, attracting many customers specifically because they are not engaged in *'inah* transactions.

In the last two or three years, there has been a strong trend towards cross-*Shari'a* jurisdictional co-operation. For instance, there may be a Saudi bank, with one idea of how to apply *Shari'a*, and a Malaysian bank, with an alternative position, co-operating in financing the same project. Perhaps they do not agree on the structure, but they may divide the project into tiers so that each may deliver what the client needs. Furthermore, AAOIFI standards are beginning to feature more prominently in the documentation, which is bringing a greater level of consensus, which is a positive move in the broader Islamic space. It serves to minimise the difference between the Islamic scholars of different countries or regions.

HSBC is an example of an institution with global Islamic finance operations. HSBC Amanah operates in many countries: Saudi Arabia, Malaysia, Brunei, Indonesia and others. Their structure is to have a central *Shari'a* board as well as local *Shari'a* boards. It is not that one is superior to another, but the local *Shari'a* board addresses the local issues. The local *Shari'a* board may permit the practise of some contracts, for instance, *'inah*, but the global *Shari'a* board will not.

This emerging standardisation is also creating an element of reputational risk for *Shari'a* scholars, especially for those who may appear to diverge from the opinion and structures that have been considered by pre-eminent scholars and either passed or rejected according to their understanding of *Shari'a*. It may be possible to launch a contentious product initially with a sufficient marketing effort, but if that product encounters problems and goes to court in an Islamic jurisdiction, then the *Shari'a* judge, when looking to determine whether the underlying structure is enforceable, will revert to *ijma'*, or consensus. AAOIFI, for lack of a better authority, is one entity that may be looked upon as the best form of reflecting *Shari'a* consensus. So, the reputational risk of not following the AAOIFI standards is quite perilous for the scholars and those entities that decide to do so. There has even been some discussion that AAOIFI may begin to approach individual scholars who are being found to issue errant opinions that are in flagrant disregard of their standards.

With respect to gaining authorisation of *Shari'a* compliance, each product is likely to vary in what is required. For structures that are well understood within a certain jurisdiction, the process can be quite quick, but sometimes, especially in a country like Spain, where maybe scholars are not familiar with the law, and the law might not be available in Arabic or English for scholars who do not understand Castellano, the process may drag on for several months. If it is a complex product, then that will result in a longer process also, requiring consultations from business people, lawyers and *Shari'a* scholars to work on the structure of the product. If it is clear and straightforward it might not take so long, but complexity generally adds time to the process.

What one can observe is that there are some *Shari'a* scholars in the old tradition, in that they have received training in *fiqh*, but they do not have a good understanding of the principles of banking and finance. They are quite capable of applying the accepted rulings according to a defined code, but in terms of developing new products it does become an impediment. In Saudi Arabia, the large majority of PhDs hold their qualifications in *Shari'a*, but very few are involved in advising the financial sector, because it is something quite complicated. What is required of these scholars is a multidisciplinary background to be in a position to advise financial institutions so that they can be the *Shari'a* aspects of their operations.

With the emergence of some consensus and standardisation in the Islamic finance industry, some may ask whether it is time to introduce some form of ratings agency for Islamic products. In fact, some years ago a *Shari'a* ratings agency was established, but it did not endure. This may have been due in part to poor management, but the impact of receiving a negative rating for any institution makes the exercise of ratings quite unpopular. Just as with credit ratings in conventional finance, the parties involved want to be sure of having the correct credit rating before entering into a contract. It is not conceivable that any institution or project could survive after receiving a rating of 'B-' from a *Shari'a* point-of-view. A lot of work was done for that institution, and a system developed adopting a neutral position, using AAA, AA, A and other ratings. It was not intended to suggest that one school was better than another or to second guess the *Shari'a* boards of any institutions, but the industry did not embrace it.

What are the Islamic restrictions on the structure of asset securitisation?

With very few *sukuk* actually being asset-backed, almost all of them being asset-backed, the question is whether it is possible to move the industry forward towards securitisation. In some places, for instance Germany, the model of securitising real assets, such as equipment or vehicles under lease, requires the creation of a small company, with owners, which creates a potential conflict of interests, meant to create an obligation in the originator. In Spain, the securitisation market had been very active, mainly with mortgages. SPVs were created that had the right to collect the payments from the mortgages. The most senior mortgages were then sold by the pool of mortgages back to investors. The originating bank would be liable for the first loss, as a means of ensuring they were not issuing bad credit. What happened in December 2007, however, has put an end to that market. Guarantees used to be issued so that the ratings agencies would give an AAA rating for the most senior bonds. While this used to be just 3 percent, it has increased to 20 per cent and, as a result, is no longer viable.

Securitisation with assets under lease provides a very good opportunity for Islamic banking. Perhaps that would be problematic for the situation described for Spain, but generally when assets are being leased there is the potential to construct an Islamic deal. There is an institution in France, engaging in the leasing of houses and other real estate, tackling this very issue. It is quite sizeable, and they are in the last stages of developing the structure. Mortgages, however, cannot be touched by Islamic banking. As long as the financing is done through lending, there is no way it can be structured Islamically to create a security or *sukuk*.

It is a very 'grey' line between asset-backed and asset-based contracts. The main consideration is whether the investors want to take on the risk of the assets themselves. In an asset-backed contract, the investors have the right and the power to seize the asset if there is a minimal default. However, speaking to Saudi bankers it is not uncommon to find that they are generally not concerned about the asset; that it is just an excuse. What they want is the guarantee of repurchase from the *sukuk* originator. Thus, not being interested in taking ownership of the assets in question, investors actually prefer asset-based. The asset is used in order to structure the deal Islamically, however, the key asset for the investor is actually the repurchase guarantee.

This was pivotal in the default of the East Cameron Partners *sukuk*, in the sense that it was not clear as to whether the *sukuk* holders could seize the assets. The US courts are quite accustomed to securitisation, and they did uphold the *sukuk* holders' rights over the assets, but it is not clear what might occur in other jurisdictions.

It is noteworthy that the above description of the difference between asset-backed and asset-based contracts pertains just to the rights of the investors over the assets. It is not the case that 'asset-based' refers to contracts concerning existing assets, thus monetising them, and that 'asset-backed' refers to new build assets. 'Asset-backed' means that the investor is taking on the asset risk themselves, and asset-based means the investor takes on the risk of the issuer, and the assets are only collateral security.

This distinction is an important one, considering the statements in 2007 of Sheik Muhammad Taqi Usmani, Chairman of the International Shari'a Council for AAOIFI, that 85 per cent of *sukuk* are *haram*, or not *Shari'a* complaint. Taqi Usmani stated that most *sukuk* are another way of monetising existing assets. This would not seem to fit well with the *maqasid al Shari'a*, the spirit, that creates something new.

One very clear and simple problem related to asset-backed contracts surrounds the issue of ownership. Consider the case of a Spanish bank, for instance, that may want to finance a Spanish infrastructure company to build a new airport in Saudi Arabia. As the airport is in Saudi Arabia, a foreign bank has no right to own any part of it, so the Spanish bank cannot buy the share of the Spanish infrastructure company. So, the resulting contract will necessarily be asset-based. The bank is notionally connected to the airport and its associated risk but does not own outright any part of it. With an asset-backed contract, the airport is divided into units, and if the airport succeeds, the owner of those units benefits, and similarly, if the airport does poorly, the owner of those units suffers as a result. However, with asset-based contracts, the bank may turn to the infrastructure company and demand compensation for the underperforming interest that it holds in the project. The project company would have to bear the losses and recompense the bank, even up to the point of their loss. So, there is a difference between ownership and collateralisation, even when it has passed the *Shari'a* test for ownership.

So it is that most investors prefer to take on the risk of the institution itself. That is where the purchase undertaking comes in, to transform, at some point, the ownership of assets into an obligation on the issuer, thus the investor is exposed to the risk of the issuer. This creates a big hurdle to Islamic finance for infrastructure companies, because most of their financing is non-recourse, so they do not have an obligation to buy the debt back. This means that it is difficult to structure 'off-balance sheet' transactions if what the investor wants in the end is the credit risk of the infrastructure company. It is a key problem.

Another problem is that most of the liquidity in Islamic banking comes from deposits in Islamic banks. Deposits are short-duration, whereas infrastructure projects are generally long-duration, so there is a mismatch between the terms of these two elements, which is another important issue to consider.

One way of structuring these projects is that the investors place their money with an investment agent. That agent, representing the investors, enters into a contract with the project company. The investment agent procures the construction of the project and leases that, on a forward basis, to the company. That is a brief summary of the structure, but fundamentally how it works is through project ownership and lease, the Islamic financiers being the owners of the project. Their remedies are eviction, as the project owner, and those remedies must flow down from that. So, it is important to make the distinction from the conventional finance approach and realise that they are not exactly the same. However, through the service agent agreement, a lot of the risks are then passed back to the project company on behalf of the project financiers.

From a guarantee point of view, it may even work better, because one of the main issues with conventional project finance is that of 'step in rights' and execution of the guarantee. If the financiers effectively own the asset, then that should make it easier to execute that guarantee in the event of non-compliance with the lease agreement. There may, however, be issues if the lease agreement is not completely linked to the interest payments of a conventional financing structure. In short, there should not be any specific problem if limited recourse financing is being applied. Full recourse financing is a different scenario because there would be some kind of unconditional repurchase agreement on the asset. But that type of financing that would be especially interesting.

The treatment of immaterial assets is quite important, since the project might not be an airport in Saudi Arabia, but a toll road in Spain, the particularity being that the toll road is owned by the government, which then issues rights to construct and operate it for a number of years. The same lease and repurchase agreement can also be used on this type of immaterial asset, which is essentially a contract with the government. As mentioned previously, this type of concession has the nature of a usufruct, which is considered sufficiently tangible for use in Islamic finance. In fact, it could be considered significantly more tangible than a transaction in which the asset under consideration were airtime for Mobile Saudi Arabia and other telecom companies.

For purposes of *sukuk* rating, can credit enhancement be used as an incentive by the government by using insurance, and can operating risk and business risk shift to a *sukuk* issuer through a repurchase agreement?

This question is related to the situation where the markets have closed, perhaps because some financiers are looking for some caution on the equity side. This caution could be provided by the government and might be a necessary step in order to reopen the market. To what extent can that kind of guarantee be used in these Islamic finance structures?

Generally, this kind of credit enhancement can be used if the government is a third party, from a contractual point of view. The government can be considered a third party who can issue such a guarantee without creating *Shari'a* problems if its ownership is less than 50 per cent. If its involvement exceeds 50 per cent it can no longer be considered a real third party, and no exception is granted for it being the government. This is despite the argument that when a private entity guarantees someone's return, the instrument begins to look like an interest-bearing loan, but when the government does so for one of its own entities, it is doing so not for its own benefit but for the public good. Moreover, there has been a lot of discussion regarding whether ownership is actually the critical aspect of making judgements on these guarantees, since management may prove to be more important. For the managers of a project, a conflict of interest may be created even though their ownership is less than 50 per cent. So, attention is now being given not only to the ownership but also to how close the two entities are and whether they are affected by the management of the other.

There is the example of the guarantee arm of the World Bank, the Multilateral Investment Guarantee Agency (MIGA). It provided a guarantee for a port project in Sudan. However, in this type of situation, if the guarantee is being provided for a fee, then there is a problem. The *fatwa* from the Fiqh Academy of the OIC provides that such a guarantee should be free and that it can only be provided by a government that has a keen interest in promoting the project. If it is to be something that is secured for a fee, then it is not difficult to secure some form of guarantee or insurance to cover the risks. That is not permissible under *Shari'a* law.

With respect to guarantees, the repurchase agreements that are commonplace in *sukuk* represent an interesting scenario. The financiers are owners of the SPV, and hence the assets of the project, which are leased back to the originator. The contracts are usually arranged so that there is a repurchase undertaking by the *sukuk* originator to buy the assets back at the end of the period of the lease agreement. Some believe that this repurchase should be agreed in principle but not at a fixed price. The argument there is that a predefined repurchase price, rather than a market price, amounts to a full guarantee. A resolution of the Fiqh Academy of the OIC does not agree with this argument, however, ruling that both a promise to buy and a promise to drift are permissible. The sale price, therefore, may be the market price, or it may be a price agreed upon when entering the contract.

How do Islamic financial entities approach due diligence in their projects?

Because of the risks associated with the transactions in Islamic banking, due diligence and in-depth analysis in Islamic finance is more important than in conventional project finance. Looking at the risk associated with any project financing in terms of operational risk, or credit risk, also late payment or non-payment risk, this obliges Islamic institutions to study the transactions more closely to ensure that the other party's obligations are within the set parameters. To do this really requires people with a good understanding of how to structure the transaction in the first place, and the analysis of the resultant cash flow projection is also an important part of the analysis. Then there is also the reputation risk, which depends on *Shari'a* and the institution itself.

The unique aspect of due diligence for Islamic finance comes from the innovation. This means that every transaction will have its own features. While this allows the institutions to really come up with something new, it can complicate the process. Moreover, everything with those transactions must pass the *Shari'a* test, so in reality the due diligence in Islamic finance is more stringent, since it incorporates all of the conventional processes plus *Shari'a*.

One piece of advice, perhaps more applicable to the feasibility stage, a first step, is that if the project and the financing are planned in a foreign country, obviously it is beneficial to speak to the central bank and the ministry of finance, or the regulation agency for capital markets in that country, just to get their opinion on *Shari'a* contracts and what the project is trying to accomplish. The laws that apply in each country will differ, and what has been done previously and agreed upon by the parties might not be applicable under the laws of that country.

One interesting case is that of an institution in US that is using *murabaha* and *ijarah* to acquire real estate for customers, either to buy or to use. If they were operating a conventional debt/credit business, as in traditional banking, they might accept lower-quality real estate, for instance having defects, because they would accept the ability of the client to pay as superior to the quality of the collateral. However, because the title will actually pass through the bank, either when it buys the registered title and passes it under *murabaha*, or when it takes ownership under *ijarah*, the required standard of the properties is higher, even though the client is creditworthy. So, there is often a layer of asset orientation which is deeper than in a traditional credit environment.

Interestingly, an exercise was conducted to create a synthetic index of Islamic banks listed in the market. After comparing this to the index of conventional banks since July 2007, it was found that Islamic banks have been outperforming by as much as 45 points. This may be linked to the kind of assets being used as collateral in Islamic finance.

Is it possible to refinance a project via Islamic finance?

There was a large, conventionally financed petrochemical project in Saudi Arabia which was the first time that that was done, so a precedent has been established. The French water company Le Syndicat des Eaux d'Ile-de-France (SEDIF) was involved in the transaction. It was a highly complicated deal, based around a structure where the Islamic investors' infusion of cash was placed in an escrow, and at closing all of the existing debt was repaid. The Islamic financiers took over part ownership of the project, and it was refinanced as an Islamically compliant structure. So, there is a precedent and, looking at it logically, does not seem to be any reason why it cannot be done. The main requirements are that care be taken with the structure, and a lot of cash!

This need not be limited to project finance. There are cases of banks that have converted from a conventional model to an Islamic structure, so much so that a process has become well established. One part of the process, of course, involves refinancing Islamically a lot of transactions that initially were financed conventionally.

One problematic situation on which *Shari'a* scholars have taken many positions is that of when someone is in debt and unable to make his payments. Some scholars adhere to the teaching of the *Qur'an* that such a person should be given sufficient time to be able to repay his obligations and, of course, the jurisprudence is rich in interpretations of this statement. Other classical scholars have held that if he is in dire need, impoverished and unable to pay, if he is able to make a transaction with another entity, then there is no problem in him entering into that contract in order to gain liquidity to repay the initial debt. Some *Shari'a* scholars have adapted this position, although most of the transactions are done with legal entities and not individuals who can suffer being in dire need. So, it has often been the practice that the indebted entity has entered into a new contract for the purpose of availing itself of liquidity in order to meet the payments due.

Can *istisna'a sukuk* become an effective way to finance green-field projects in PPPs again?

Istisna'a sukuk has been considered to be *sukuk* for green-field projects, being used when a project is a new construction. When an existing structure or asset is being leveraged against the generated cash flows, then an *ijarah* agreement is more common. In 2007, Sheik Usmani stated that the promise of a fixed repurchase price under *istisna'a* is not *Shari'a* complaint, and this has led to the issuance of *istisna'a sukuk* disappearing from the market.

The Al-Waha case has been a useful teaching case for many years because, although it involves payment being received for construction to be completed in the future, the essence of *istisna'a*, it does so using an alternative to the *sukuk* contracts; in this case *musharaka* with *ijarah mausufah fi dhimmah*. This is superior to issuing *sukuk* to *istisna'a* on its own. Note that the *ijarah mausufah fi dhimmah*, with or without *musharaka*, also incorporates *istisna'a* for the procurement with the contractor. With better methodologies, such as this, it should not be necessary to return to a structure of disputed validity.

For a Spanish construction company that wins a greenfield construction contract in Saudi Arabia, seeking a suitable structure to finance the project before it enters into operation, *musharaka* represents a better methodology. However, as mentioned earlier, it is linked to the company's status either as just a contractor or as co-owner. As a co-owner, the *musharaka* with *ijarah mausufah fi dhimmah* is preferable. As a contractor only, using *istisna'a*, there is a cost involved, and that is illiquidity, because it would not be a tradable instrument.

Pure *istisna'a sukuk* can be problematic because initially, from a *Shari'a* point-of-view, it is a form of debt. It is an obligation on the contractor to deliver certain assets according to the specification and therefore cannot be traded. However, if the issuer of the *sukuk* also owns the land, for instance, and wants to transfer the ownership of the land with the *istisna'a* part, then the *istisna'a sukuk* would be tradeable since, from day one, it represents a real asset.

Adopting a *musharaka*-based structure will result in the project company taking a share in the ownership of the project assets, and therefore it will share those risks, as well as the rewards; similar in some ways to venture capital. However, AAOIFI has made allowances to realign the risks and rewards to a certain degree. For example, a profit-sharing ratio could be established which appears to favour one party, and the other party would be held to that agreement, especially if the targets are not being met. However, if the targets are being exceeded, the favoured party may be prepared to allow any windfall over and above the expected benchmark to be paid to the other as a form of bonus, all of which could be documented. Such an arrangement would appear to have the characteristics of preferred stock, but it is not quite the same.

The idea of preferred stock has often been raised, but it cannot be done in Islamic finance, and therefore venture capital is also outside the sphere of Islamic finance. What is done is that, instead of a 'distribution waterfall', with a tiered structure, there is a single-layer structure. That is how it is possible to have the same rights as a preferred shareholder, but without the priority in distribution. However, it is possible to alter the profit-sharing ratio according to the achievement, or not, of certain defined milestones. Graphically, that could be represented by a line, the gradient of which indicates the ratio of the cash flow distribution between the parties; however, at some point, when a particular cash flow is achieved, the slope of that line changes, reflecting a different profit-sharing ratio. So, that is how something similar to a preferred share situation could be reproduced Islamically, by altering the distributions throughout the history of the project.

The forward lease construct of *ijarah mausufah fi dhimmah* is built on the premise that payments are being made during the construction. Once the project is complete, these payments should result in some kind of credit corresponding to the advance rent payments. The reality is that this credit quite often ends up not as a real credit, but as a book entry that, at the end of the project, is recouped via a commensurate adjustment in the rent, which itself may bring up some longer-term concerns. Those advance rent payments are always contingent on the completion of the project and must be returned if the project is not delivered. Often, however, the commercial intention is not to have to return that money because there is a cost. For this reason, it may be beneficial to reconsider a way to re-characterise, or recalibrate, those funds in a way that creates a longer-term interest on the financiers' part.

It is true that repaying those advanced rent payments does create some problems for some bankers, and there are moves in the housing industry, using the same basic structure, to include something else whereby what used to be advance rent is no longer known as that and does not have to be repaid, which some would say appears to be a more fair way.

How can Islamic countries benefit from Spanish expertise in financing renewable energy infrastructure projects?

In Granada, in the south of Spain, a Spanish company is building thermo-solar power plants, storing the heat energy from the sun in molten salt. It seems that Granada is the best place in Spain to locate such a plant. However, they say that the potential output of such a plant in Saudi Arabia is as much as four times greater. It would seem, therefore, to be a perfect marriage. The Spanish have developed considerable expertise in the field of renewable energy, and the Saudis have liquidity to finance those types of projects. Furthermore, with the creation of new power plants and infrastructure, the projects are well-suited to the asset-based financing structures that have been developed by Islamic finance.

One good place to start, as a Spanish developer, is to approach the Saudi Arabian Government Investment Agency (SAGIA). Its role is to identify projects of this type, and solar power would obviously be one of its priorities. That is not to say that it will be a simple task. The Saudis are not very familiar with any type of energy except oil, so the market for renewable energy needs to be created. Such projects are complicated, and although there is experience of megaprojects in the Gulf, they are even more complicated, requiring much expertise and financing.

It is noteworthy, however, that, even though the intensity of solar radiation in Saudi Arabia is much higher than in the best location in Spain, solar energy is still unlikely to be efficient enough to achieve price parity with the existing grid. Therefore, what would be required would be a legal framework with guarantees, be that through power-purchase agreements, some type of take-off agreement, government grants or tariff subsidies in order ensure the use of the power being generated and an adequate return from its sale. The technology may continue to evolve, but today, even with that high level of solar radiation, it will be very difficult to find projects that could be viable by themselves without any type of further injection of money over and above the market price of electricity.

The potential market for renewable energy is huge, and even in Saudi Arabia people are beginning to think seriously about the local consumption of oil. Oil is sold at unbelievable prices, so it does not benefit the people of Saudi Arabia to be consuming a large proportion of their own production. Perhaps there will come a time when prices rise and alternative sources of energy, such as solar, become economical. However, for Spain to be a serious player in this field in the Middle East, it needs to come up with a total solution. It is difficult to focus on just one part if the other parts are not available.

The government in Saudi Arabia has been making loans of billions of riyals to electricity companies, and there are those who believe that there will be a shortage if heavy investments are not made. Similarly, there have been calls for greater incentives and subsidies for renewable energy. This is a worldwide trend, and Spain has developed an expertise that can be exported all over the world, not just in the Middle East. Moreover, if someone wants to invest Islamically in such a project, wherever it is in the world, a structure can be found to accommodate it. Selling the idea in the West may be easier, since the demand for renewable energy seems to be higher due to the desire to reduce dependence on Middle Eastern oil, but it is also possible to attract Islamic investors to finance those projects and have a combination of the two. Even the World Bank is pushing renewable energy, even in the developing world, and nearly every country is producing policy papers on these subjects. It is a great market for the Spanish, and with Islamic financing the Gulf could be an important source of liquidity.

King Abdulaziz University, which has been very well represented in this symposium, has a project to develop solar energy and power plants and has a sizeable budget to do so. The interest exists, and Spain is well positioned to do something. Spain also has the advantage over some other countries in that relations between Spain and the Arab world have no skeletons in the closet. The history is open, and Spain is looked upon as having a special place because of that shared history.

There is a nice example of a public–private partnership in solar energy which addresses some of the questions of miscued incentives. It is not always necessary to take money from the Middle East. This example involves the Asian Development Bank and the Japanese Fund for Cooperation in village-level solar panel installations where grid connections do not exist. The pilot scheme has been running in Bangladesh.

Those PPP structures need not be limited to renewable energy projects either. Railway projects in Saudi Arabia and the Middle East, for example, can also be financed with these structures, which are very popular at the moment. There is a lot of infrastructure spending in the Gulf region, and Spanish companies should be well positioned to seek out that business. If they do their homework and try to achieve Islamic-compliant financing structures, that would give them an even greater advantage.

This discussion has covered many of the topics of how Spanish companies and other Western entities can introduce themselves to Islamic finance and begin to use those financing structures for large infrastructure projects. The adoption of those tools will allow those Western companies to access funding tied up in the Islamic world and will be very useful in improving relations between East and West.

4

The Legal and Tax Adaptation of Islamic Finance Instruments in Spain

Symposium workshop

IE Business School, Madrid, Spain, 17th June 2010

Chairmen

Ahmed Belouafi, Researcher, Islamic Economics Research Centre, King Abdulaziz University, Saudi Arabia
Guillermo Canalejo, Attorney, Uría and Menéndez, Spain
Abderrazak Belabes, Researcher, Islamic Economics Research Centre, King Abdulaziz University, Saudi Arabia
Alfredo Cabellos, Senior Associate, Uría and Menéndez, Spain

Special Comments made by

Gilles Saint Marc, Gide Loyrette Nouel A.A.R.P.I., France

The goal of this discussion, first of all, is to have an introduction to the issues, from a legal and tax perspective, with respect to Islamic finance. It may be assumed that there are differing levels of knowledge, so it will be endeavoured to raise the level to a minimum standard and discuss the different contracts and the different ways that the *Shari'a* principles of finance may be treated and then consider, from a civil law point of view, how those structures can be adapted within the legal system. Ultimately, the goal is to understand how to make Islamic finance available to Western enterprises that want to invest in assets that need, or want, to be financed with *Shari'a*-compliant funds, the issuance of *sukuk* and all of those instruments which are becoming increasingly familiar.

Islamic finance emerged in the 1960s and 1970s to serve the needs of some Muslims who refrained from using the services offered by the mainstream financial system. At that time, Islamic finance became an international phenomenon that has since spread to almost all regions of the world. It is no longer something that is confined to Muslims only but is here for everyone to examine and to see how its use and introduction as part of the conventional system can be beneficial. The elements are particularly significant in this respect: the classification of sources of finance, innovation and financial inclusion.

The process of introducing Islamic finance faces some legal and tax hurdles. In order to open up those issues and create a level of understanding that will help in the advancement of Islamic finance, the following ten open questions have been posed to guide the discussion.

1. Why this topic?
   To initiate the discussion on the appropriate platform, it is interesting first to explore:

   • The different principles and modes of finance between conventional and Islamic finance.
   • The legal and tax implications of Islamic finance, creating a level playing field, and removing uncertainty and providing clarity to lay the foundation for an enabling environment to send positive signals for concerned investors.

2. Who should be involved?
   Regulatory bodies, the Islamic finance industry and legal consultancy firms, if necessary. These could also include *Shari'a* scholars from bodies such as the International Fiqh Academy of the Organisation of the Islamic Conference (OIC), the Accounting and Auditing Organisation for Islamic Financial Institutions (AAOIFI) and the Islamic Financial Services Board (IFSB).

3. How to go about it?
   By ensuring that the government plays a primary role, through the appointment of an expert group to identify opportunities

and barriers, and the involvement of other stakeholders, for example, experts from the Muslim community in Spain.

4. What are the financial regulatory bodies in Spain?
   The central bank, Comisión Nacional del Mercado de Valores (CNMV), the Treasury and insurance regulators, among others.

5. What can be learnt from other experiments?
   There has been a variety of models and approaches, including those of the UK, France and Lebanon. In brief, what are the positive and negative factors of these approaches? Does Spain just copy or begin from where others had stopped?

6. What is the nature of Spanish law, and can a suitable model be designed to introduce Islamic finance?

7. What are the various modes of finance and types of institutions of Islamic finance and how can they be accommodated?
   Murabaha, *ijarah*, *mudaraba*, retail and wholesale banking, *takaful* insurance, Islamic funds.

8. Are there existing instruments in the Spanish legal framework that are close in their nature and purpose to Islamic funds?

9. How would an Islamic bank apply for a license in Spain?

10. When will Spain be ready to accommodate Islamic finance?
    Drawing a road map for the whole process so that positive steps are taken in the near future.

To give a short introduction to the principles of Islamic finance, the main principle is the prohibition of *riba*, which is, basically, the charging of interest. The lending of money, by itself, cannot be remunerated simply due to the passing of time. This concept has existed in other civilisations besides Islam. Historically, both Christianity and Judaism have condemned the lending of money with interest, a practice known as 'usury'. The Judeo-Christian world has developed such that the charging of interest is commonplace. It is interesting to see, however, that under Spanish law's civil code, it is understood that a loan does not yield interest, although this is not the case under the commercial code; a significant difference. So under the civil code, unless the parties expressly state that interest should be paid, loans are regarded as interest-free.

Obviously, the prohibition of *riba* under Islamic law does not mean that financing cannot be granted. What it means is that it must be provided in a different way, which is for the financier to participate with the borrower in the production of income, in the yield of a profit, either from joining in the business being financed or in the ownership of an asset that is being leased or sold, to either the borrower or another party. The difference is that the lender will become either a partner in the business, will become a supplier of services in the form of leasing assets or will become a seller of assets to the final client.

There is a transformation, when compared to conventional finance, in that the lender is no longer a passive investor providing the funds; that is the lendder must engage with the borrower and, to some extent, share the profit and losses resulting from the business of the borrower, or through the exploitation of the assets which are subject to financing.

Accordingly, from a legal point of view, the substance remains the same, in the sense that the interests of the lender and borrower, to make funds available for investment in a business or in assets, are still present. There is a financial objective for both parties, but it is transformed into a different type of agreement. It is transformed into a leasing agreement, a purchase-and-sale agreement, a joint ownership of assets or a joint venture. That means that the format, as it would be seen from a Western perspective, does not coincide that well with the objective, with the goal of the contract, which is to finance the client and borrower.

This is especially interesting and complicated from a tax law point of view, which primarily follows the format of the contracts, because the contracts yield certain types of income, which are taxed differently, depending on how they are generated. The taxation of interest is different from the taxation of a dividend, which is different from the taxation of a business profit, which is different from the taxation of a gain resulting from the sale of the asset. So, one of the most difficult steps, and where reform is necessary, is in the adaptation of the conventional tax structures to Islamic finance products, which have a different legal form and contract, but which are intended to provide the same financing and the same sort of interest yield to the lender, albeit in the form of rents or profits.

Also relevant, from a tax point of view, is the fact that underlying Islamic financial instruments are assets or businesses; hence indirect taxation is very important. In the EU, and therefore in Spain, indirect taxation is applicable every time an asset is transferred, in the form of either VAT or transfer tax. Depending on how the transaction is conducted, and who is conducting the transaction, those taxes may be an extra cost. In many of the Islamic financial instruments that are typically used, there is double taxation on transfer tax or there is double taxation on stamp duties. That means that, in comparison with conventional Western finance, Islamic finance instruments are not on the same playing field, since there is a higher degree of taxation on Islamic financial products than for a standard loan agreement due to the form of the contracts. So, there is a conflict between the form and the goal of these Islamic contracts, since obviously they will be compared with Western finance contracts under Western tax norms. With this added penalty of double taxation, Islamic finance cannot be efficient; thus, it will always be too expensive and not competitive.

The situation in France, where much work has been done on reforming the tax system to accommodate Islamic finance, is very interesting and likely to prove to be a useful example for Spain and many other civil law countries. This can be outlined by posing three questions: Where did they come from? Where do they stand today? What are the next steps forward?

The formation of an Islamic Finance Committee was instigated by the French Minister of Finance, Christine Lagarde, in January 2008. A group of about 40 people, including lawyers, bankers and scholars, was formed with the mission of identifying the legal and tax obstacles that prevented the accommodation of Islamic finance into the French financial system. The preliminary conclusions were rendered in June 2008 and were three-fold.

The first conclusion was that there are many analogous principles between Islamic finance and French law. This may be a result of the fact that usury was prohibited in France, even between professionals, until 2003. It is certainly related to the common attitude towards uncertainty and speculation, which is a basic principle of French law and is fairly common in civil law countries. It is important to make very clear that the fact that the principles underlying Islamic finance do not belong exclusively to Islam; they are common principles that were assessed and incorporated by the French system in the thirteenth century. It appears that the crisis of conventional finance has made Islamic finance attractive again and particularly relevant, but one could argue that it is simply up to conventional finance to become responsible again. These common principles were the first conclusion.

The second conclusion was the realisation that within the existing framework there were many 'tools in the tool box' that would allow the practice of Islamic finance. In other words, Islamic finance was already being practised without anyone realising it. For example, *ijarah* is basically leasing, mutual funds would fit with *mudaraba* and participating loans could be considered either *mudaraba* or *musharaka*. The same is probably true of other countries; Islamic finance is already present without conscious realisation of it. The tools exist, and the key is to be aware of them and flag them.

The third and final point was that there is a need for clarification. Sometimes things are not so clear, and there needs to be some technical regulation to clarify that a convention or regulation from a given code actually fulfils certain requirements of the Islamic context. Of course, the key is the tax aspect and making sure that conventional and Islamic finance are on the same level and that there is no particular competitive disadvantage to Islamic finance.

France's interest in Islamic finance is driven by three things. The first is pragmatism. The global financial crisis created a large demand for liquidity, and there is much liquidity in the Middle East. Being pragmatic, or opportunistic, is simply a matter of fact. The second point, where Islamic finance is interesting for the long term, is the principles underlying Islamic finance. Simplicity, long-term financing and the participative nature of financing, where the financier is not gaining income merely from the passage of time but is associated with the risks of the generated cash flows of his investment, is an interesting and entrepreneurial approach. The third point is the idea of not playing in the casino of the financial markets but financing the real economy and tangible assets. All of these will be very interesting, whatever the recovery of the Interbank or the conventional bond market will be in.

It should not be overlooked, either, that France has the largest Muslim population in Europe. There are about six million Muslims in France, which is about three times the Muslim population of the UK. One argument, which is difficult to assess precisely, is that introducing Islamic finance is a way to integrate the Muslim population and will not necessarily drive communitarianism; however, views on that differ.

Several elements define where France stands today. With respect to funds, there is an EU Directive, 'Undertakings for Collective Investments in Transferrable Securities', which for most assets completely fits the principle of *mudaraba*. So, whenever a private equity fund is investing in the equity of companies which are engaged in *halal* activities and conform to certain financial ratios, it satisfies the criteria of *mudaraba*. This was clarified in July 2007 by the issue of a specific recommendation by Autorité des Marchés Financiers (AMF), the French stock market regulator, basically stating that *Shari'a* indexed mutual funds are compliant with French law and provide for some percentage in terms of clarification of non-pure dividends. *Sukuk* is more difficult in terms of *fiqh* regime. Attempts to pass specific legislation have not been successful, and hence it has been decided to work out something with the existing tools, which presumably will include the securitisation framework, although the securitisation of cash flow does not fit the definition of *sukuk* per se. By combining it with *fiducie*, which is a French trust, the ownership of the underlying assets is transferred to the *sukuk* holder. This is underway, and a structure memo has been sent to AAOIFI in Bahrain and is in consultation with international scholars.

A technical regulation on the prospectus format, an AMF regulation of July 2008, was issued to explain how the EU regulation prospectus should be adjusted to take account of *sukuk*, which were not contemplated at the time, depending on whether these are asset-based or asset-backed *sukuk*. There is another regulation, from the NYSE Euronext, Paris, from July 2009, which sets out the steps necessary for listing *sukuk* on Euronext. In February 2009, a tax instruction was issued regarding the extent to which remuneration which is paid under *sukuk* can be assimilated, for tax purposes, as interest of debt instruments. Of course, *sukuk* is not a debt instrument but represents a co-ownership right to a pool of assets. However, certain conditions have been defined under which the tax administration accepts the principle of this remuneration being tax deductible for the issuer and with no resulting tax for non-French investors.

Real-estate finance usually takes the form of *murabaha*, which is the double transfer of assets. Instead of the end purchaser borrowing the money from the bank in the conventional way and purchasing the property and repaying the bank over time, the Islamic bank purchases the property and re-sells it to the end purchaser on a deferred payment basis, which is economically identical to conventional finance. It is easy to see the problems that this arrangement immediately raises. There are legal problems associated with the bank becoming a vendor and with their warranty obligations in that role. There is also the problem of the double transfer duties, which in France are 5.09 per cent of the value of the underlying asset, so they are not trivial. The idea is to neutralise these double transfer duties, as has been done in the UK, so that it is only necessary to pay once.

With respect to the next steps, *sukuk* is clearly one piece of the Islamic finance puzzle. It is also important to set in place the other pieces, all of which need to be sound in order to have a global framework which fits Islamic finance. Once thing that is very important is the memorandum of understanding that has been signed between the Paris EUROPLACE, the financial markets organisation, and AAOIFI, the international organisation in Bahrain that produces standards. As of July 2010, 20 AAOIFI standards had been translated from Arabic to French so that French finance professionals can really understand what is being discussed. It is nice to talk about *mudaraba* and *musharaka* and related subjects, but it is even better to have standard forms that are fairly commonly accepted, and not to have to work from English translations, which can be misleading; for instance, when they refer to English law concepts like trusts, which do not exist in Spain or France. There is still much work to be done, but the initial focus has been on the 20 key standards.

New tax instructions to coincide with those standards, two of them specifically related to *istisna'a* and *ijarah*, may prove to be very useful for project finance and public–private partnerships (PPPs) since *istisna'a* is usually used for the construction phase, and *ijarah* for the operation. There are also other tax instructions specifically relating to *mudaraba*, *wakalah* and *salam*.

Another memorandum of understanding is in place between the Qatar Islamic Bank (QIB) and a major savings bank in France, BPCE, which may lead to the creation of an Islamic retail bank. There is a lot of interest in these developments in France. French SMEs really need equity funding, and many of them are carrying out *halal* activities. Therefore it could be a 'win-win' solution and also a way to train people from the Gulf about how the private equity industry works, how to select companies and what their roles should be on the boards of directors. It is not only just asking them for their money, but also providing them with training and development.

Takaful is one Islamic finance concept that is on the table, and it would appear that the existing mutual regime fits that definition, but it encounters practical problems in the EU framework. The EU Insurance Directive requires that *takaful* or mutual companies invest in certain eligible instruments, but at present, at the EU level, these instruments are mostly real estate assets and interest-bearing instruments. That is where *takaful* does not work. Moreover, the *sukuk* market is not yet well developed, so even if the EU regulation were to change, it would not be possible to replace the invested insurance premiums into *Shari'a*-compliant instruments.

Three pieces of advice that come out of the French experience would be as follows. Begin by setting up a committee of professionals from different disciplines – law, taxation, banking and scholarship – to investigate the issues. Perhaps one mistake of the French experience was in not engaging sufficiently with scholars in the early stages. At the end of the day, everything must be validated by Islamic scholars and will be the subject of *fatwa*. It is important that all of the stakeholders are represented in the committee, and auditing the legal and tax situation is a good place to start in order to know what needs to be adjusted and prioritised.

Avoiding legislation, where possible, is highly advisable, and where possible, it is better to work through regulation, tax instructions and such things. Going before the parliament is a painful exercise. First, because there are many big issues today, and the parliament cannot do everything at the same time, and, second, there is a risk that some will say that it is the end of the neutrality of the state and that it is the introduction of Islam in Western countries. Therefore, the more expedient measure is to avoid legislation and adapt what is already in place.

The last piece of advice would be to pursue the translation of standards into the local language. Islamic finance is a very interesting field, but it can be difficult to understand, and it is easier to educate people and disseminate the concepts when they are translated into

Spanish, for example. AAOIFI would most likely be pleased to sign a similar agreement to that made by the French with the committee of whichever country was interested in taking steps to open their financial system to Islamic finance.

There are many different contracts available in Islamic finance, but they are derived from a limited number of standard types that often can be summarised quite simply. *Musharaka*, for example, is simply a partnership agreement, whereas *ijarah* is just a leasing agreement with the condition that the lessor owns the goods or the assets for the duration of the contract until the end of the lease. If it is a lease-to-own, which means that on maturity the ownership is transferred to the lessee, it could be a 'diminishing *musharaka*', where the lessee would gradually own an increasing share of the assets throughout the duration of the contract, resulting in a full ownership at maturity. *Mudaraba* is a kind of partnership where one party contributes money or capital, while the other party provides labour or manages the project, rather than putting in his own money. If both parties are contributing capital, it would be a *musharaka* contract. *Salam* is the opposite of a deferred sale, which is when the financier purchases the assets and sells them to the client on a deferred-payment basis. *Salam* is the opposite; the financier provides money now for assets delivered in the future. *Istisna'a* is a kind of construction contract, and it is a combination of hybrid lease and *salam*. The constructor provides material and work for assets to be delivered in the future. The price could be in instalments, or it could be up-front. That is the difference between *salam* and *istisna'a*; *salam* contracts require the payment to be up-front, whereas in *istisna'a* it may be deferred.

Sukuk comes in many different varieties, but there are two most common examples. One is used simply to securitise existing assets. The sale of debt is not allowed in Islamic finance, but a bank can securitise leased assets because the bank keeps the ownership of the assets and therefore can sell these leased assets to investors. If the bank also has a portfolio of sale, which becomes debts after the sale contract is signed, then the pragmatic solution is to have the debt kept below 50 per cent of the portfolio value and tangible assets making up majority. There are different views on what is the minimum and maximum debt in a portfolio; some would demand less than 30 per cent, while others would accept up to 49 per cent. That is one way to do *sukuk* – securitising an existing portfolio and selling it to investors.

Another way to do it is to initiate the transaction with the investors directly. One common form is sale and leaseback, which is the subject of many complications and debates but is probably well known in the conventional legal system. A company or bank would sell an asset and lease it back, usually lease-to-own. This is widely practised, although from a *Shari'a* point-of-view there are still some questions surrounding it.

It is very interesting to see what has been done in France. However, for banks and companies that would like to consider launching Islamic financial products or *Shari'a*-compliant financing, there are many questions. For lawyers, the main concern is certainty, not only at the regulatory level but also at the institutional level. Banks will have to take on *Shari'a* boards to vet their products, which is a new experience for them. Companies will have to contract *Shari'a* scholars to approve their projects for financing. Finding those advisors, especially those who are familiar with both *Shari'a* law and, for example, Spanish law, could prove difficult.

With respect to certainty, one key question for lawyers is whether the products will be governed by the laws of the state, for instance, France or Spain, with a *fatwa* stating that the agreement is in compliance with *Shari'a* or that it will go one step further and be governed entirely by Islamic principles. The famous Shamil v. Beximco case in London, although complex, concluded with the Court of Appeal of London disregarding an English law agreement which referred to the law as interpreted by Islamic principles. It was considered that Islamic principles were not sufficiently clearly defined and the agreement reflected different schools of thought. A specific practice group was formed on this subject by the French Islamic finance committee, which concluded that the law of the state must take precedence. Islamic finance should be governed by the laws of the state with the support of *fatwa*, something like a pre-sale report from a ratings agency. A *Shari'a* board is capable of concluding whether what has been drafted to be governed by the local law is, in addition, also complaint with *Shari'a*. Such a route is safer than choosing to ignore the local law in favour of Islamic principles, which may serve adequately until there is a dispute and the local courts fail to enforce it.

It is important to attract the support of public authorities because they also need to be involved. For the state, much infrastructure investment is required; for example, hospitals, railways and schools. These types of asset-based project, which require financing, are *Shari'a* compliant and therefore could be financed through *sukuk*, which is a certificate of co-ownership and something that would not be considered within the public deficit of the state according to the Maastricht criteria. Many countries in Europe are having trouble at present, and if they want to maintain a certain level of investment by public entities, the state and regional municipalities, then Islamic finance could be a very good way to do that. What is important is that there be a real tangible asset which is *Shari'a* compliant. So, construction, highways and project finance are all eligible as underlying assets of *sukuk* issuance. It is something that can be used tomorrow everywhere; it is not theoretical and is very relevant.

One point to keep in mind is the common ground that exists surrounding these products. Western legal instruments have evolved in a different way, perhaps in a more sophisticated way, but the basics of those Islamic instruments are still within the legal system. For example, *mudaraba* seems very complicated, but in reality it is not. It is a partnership, which is very simple to understand. While the name may be complicated, the instrument itself is not. The *mudaraba* partnership comprises a general partner who is managing the business, his own business, and a limited partner, of sorts, who is providing funds to the general partner to use to generate profits, either from the business or from the exploitation of assets. The limited partner, or silent partner, is obviously bearing the risks and rewards of the business along with the general partner. If the business is not profitable, the silent partner will also not be remunerated. He will be remunerated if the business is successful, depending on how the two partners have agreed to share the profits.

This description resembles a Spanish instrument called *la cuenta en participación*, or, in English, a joint account agreement. In the same way, the investor, the *cuenta participe*, will be remunerated according to the profit-sharing agreement that has been established, but also stands to suffer a loss if the business is not successful. These instruments are not highly used, since today it would be more usual to incorporate a limited liability company to achieve the same result, but for other reasons. The practice may have evolved away from the use of these tools, but they exist within the legal system.

In this type of arrangement, from the Spanish taxation point of view, the silent partner has a hybrid position. Providing funds to the business, he has something of the nature of a lender, but he is being remunerated on the basis of the profits of the business, something like an entrepreneur. This hybrid position is interesting from the taxation perspective because it must be decided what has preference; is the silent partner's remuneration essentially the interest that he receives as a lender, or is it a profit he receives from a business undertaken? It depends whether the system is inclined more to the lending side or the partnership side, to interest income or dividend income.

As interest income, it would be tax deductible for the business, but it probably would be remunerated in a more strenuous way. As business profit income, it would be treated differently. This is very relevant when the silent partner is a non-Spanish resident tax-payer, because the regime can be very different. The answer to this question is so unclear that the tax treatment of joint account agreements in Spain has changed three times in the last 20 years.

This concept of joint account agreement would seem to be quite flexible and to have many possibilities, especially as it is currently perceived as a debt instrument, therefore giving that tax benefit. The transaction would not incur VAT or transfer tax because there is no asset being transferred, and the investor can participate as a capital provider.

It seems that these are complicated instruments, and certain implementations are very exotic. The answer, probably, is to go back to basics, taking the simplest forms that have evolved in a complex manner. Finding the essence of these instruments in the existing legal system must be preferable to creating a new, parallel legal system, which would surely add complication and confusion. There are shared principles at the root of these contracts; what is needed is to redefine them from the legal, tax, regulatory and financial points of view.

Speaking of change and evolution, it is perhaps important to see how Islamic finance is changing as Spain and France are trying to bring in Islamic investments. An important discussion taking place is the 'form versus substance' debate. For example, considering something like *sukuk*, especially after the defaults, the dispute is over whether investors actually owned the underlying assets. This is a very fundamental issue, because when it goes to the court and it comes out that the assets were actually just playing a ceremonial role, and the investors did not really own the asset, then there is a problem. The industry is already favouring asset-backed structures where, in theory, the investors actually own the assets, and if the issuer, or the originator, fails to make the payments, then the investors can seize the assets and do as they please with them. This change in the direction in Islamic finance is something that should be taken into account at this stage.

The definition of *sukuk* has been the subject of debate, even among Islamic scholars, since Sheik Usmani declared in November 2007 that 85 per cent of *sukuk* were not *Shari'a* compliant because of the guarantee of repurchase at a nominated price, thus removing any real risk. Furthermore, the default of various *sukuk*, not least of all that of East Cameron Partners, has created much uncertainty over asset-based or asset-backed *sukuk* and the claims of *sukuk* holders over the assets. So, it is important to keep things updated, and this is why it is important to have scholars, preferably two pre-eminent international scholars from the Middle East and one local scholar who understands the local environment and which will make the connection between the two worlds. It does seem that the Islamic finance industry lost sight of the principle of *sukuk* somewhat with all these *sukuk* which were later ruled *haram*.

Looking at the market share of asset-backed *sukuk*, it is just less than 2 per cent, even though it is argued to be the more ideal *Shari'a* instrument. When asked why this is the case, bankers usually respond that the investors to whom they are going currently are not interested in securitisation structures. What they want is a structure similar to unsecured bond issuance. So, it can be seen that besides the asset type and the regulatory environment, investors do play a role in what types of instrument are in the market, because of what they are willing to buy.

A development in the European market that could possibly be explored, besides just asset-backed securities, is something like a covered bond. Asset-backed securities are 'off-balance sheet' financing, whereas a covered bond would offer that 'on-balance sheet' option; not necessarily a true sale, but giving the investors the protection of a ring-fenced asset. However, the flip side of that argument is that covered bonds are debt instruments, which may be secured a particular way, with legal priority on some underlying assets; however this is not something that really fits the definition of *sukuk*. At the end of the day, the bond holders are creditors of the issuer and not owners of an underlying asset.

Another problem that can arise for Islamic banking is the EU directive regarding the deposit-guarantee scheme. It is generally considered to be designed to maintain public order, but it basically ensures that any depositor shall get his money back. The new tax instructions issued in France regarding *murabaha*, profit-sharing investments, have been reviewed by the Banque de France and by the French Banking Commission to ensure that it works with those deposit-guarantee schemes. These instructions do not deal purely with tax aspects but also explain the product, the way it is understood, the way it will conform to the tax regime and regulations. In a profit-sharing investment account, where the money is invested in some *murabaha* or *shari'a*-compliant assets, the question is, what happens if the bank goes bust?

The deposit-guarantee schemes are funds that have received contributions from all of the banks so that there is cash available to reimburse clients, up to a certain amount, their deposit in the event of a bank going bankrupt, so the public does not suffer a loss as a result, or so that the loss will be diminished. However, in Islamic banking, it is expected that the customer of the bank shares not only in the profit, but also in the losses, of the institution that is managing his money, obviously on a *halal* basis. That means that in the event of the bank going bust and suffering a total loss, the customers ought also to share that loss. What happens, however, is that the regulators become involved and insist that the customer be protected. Surely, it is relevant that Islamic principles are preserved, but then there are also certain local laws, and public order must be maintained. That means that regardless of the principle and the terms and agreements of the bank, the customer is entitled and should be compensated from the deposit-guarantee scheme.

This has affected the Islamic Bank of Britain (IBB) in the UK, which appears to have taken an unusual point of view on the matter – that the 'truly Muslim' depositor will share the risk of the bank, as required by the profit-sharing aspects of Islamic banking, and therefore will not enforce the deposit-guarantee scheme in the event of the bank collapsing. The position in France is quite different, which is that the customer shall only get back what the money has produced in terms of investment and revenue, and if the bank fails then the customer will only receive what he would have had if it had not defaulted. The idea of the deposit-guarantee scheme is that the customer shall not assume the risk of the bank, so the customer is taking only the risk of the underlying assets into which his money has been invested. This is permitted because the money the customer has deposited is invested into underlying assets. So, if it is a *mudaraba*, where the customer contributes his money and the bank contributes its expertise, as a *mudarib*, in investing the money, the customer retains an almost direct link with the underlying assets into which his money has been invested.

With respect to the Islamic Bank of Britain, it would appear that it was actually the Financial Services Authority (FSA) that pushed towards this solution. The scholars were working very hard on an alternative, but this was the compromise that had to be made in order to be granted the licence. Nevertheless, the Islamic Bank of Britain now has a new deposit product based on *wakalah*, which actually fulfils the *Shari'a* requirements and meets the conditions of the FSA. It is important to note that Islamic banking is developing rapidly; there are new solutions and new ideas emerging all the time, and scholars are adapting to understand the regulation in the West. The first solution of IBB was something determined five years ago, but that does not mean that it is still the best solution. Things are always being done to develop new products within the existing legislation, trying to reach that compromise of something that is *Shari'a* compliant and still fulfils the legal requirements of the country in which it is offered.

What these deposit-guarantee scheme problems seem to overlook is that there are many ways to insure, and there are Islamic alternatives. There is nothing wrong with protecting deposits through the appropriate structures, for instance, a *takaful* mechanism. There are already many capital protected funds that have been initiated by Islamic banks, so really there should be no problem. In Malaysia, there is deposit insurance in place, set up by the central bank, and it actually includes a scheme for Islamic banks. As there is no issue with third-party guarantees on *mudaraba*, there is no problem with it; so this is one way to manage this concern on public order. Moreover, what some banks do, at an operational level, with *mudaraba* deposits is to set up a reserve called a 'profit equalisation reserve', which is used to smoothen the profit payment made to depositors.

Looking at deposit products in Islamic banking, there are two situations that bear consideration. The first is that the bank suffers some minor losses, which it will usually cover itself from the capital it has. The deposit-guarantee scheme will only come into play if the bank suffers a big loss or a big liquidity issue and is basically bankrupt.

In the case of the IBB, the documentation was prepared, which included the terms and conditions of the *mudaraba* contract. If, at that time, the FSA had allowed IBB to proceed with the terms and conditions as drafted, which did not include any specific statement regarding the deposit guarantee, then the contract would have been 100 percent *Shari'a* compliant. In the event that the bank suffered some small loss, it would be allowed, even from a *Shari'a* point-of-view, to compensate the client, but only as long as it is not stated in the contract. That is very important. *Shari'a* compliance in terms of banking and financial institutions means that the contract should fulfil the *Shari'a* requirements and does not contain anything that is expressly prohibited. Therefore, if in the *mudaraba* contract IBB included a statement that in the event of a loss the bank would provide compensation from its own capital, then the contract would no longer be *Shari'a* compliant. The irony here is that the FSA pushed IBB to include something in the contract that made it non-*Shari'a* compliant, but the requirements of that clause were something that the bank would have done itself anyway.

It is only when the bank actually goes bankrupt that the deposit guarantee scheme comes into operation. If the bank is bankrupt then, like any other bank, the scheme comes in to reimburse the deposit customers of the bank, which is completely *Shari'a* compliant because it is a guarantee from a third party. Understanding the situation and analysing it correctly from a *Shari'a* point of view are essential in determining what can and cannot be done. If the FSA had let IBB proceed with the normal *mudaraba* contract as drafted, it would have fulfilled the legal requirement and the *Shari'a* requirement, but due to a lack of understanding they pushed to make it non-*Shari'a* compliant. The situation at several of the large banks in the UK has been analysed, and none of them mentions in the terms and conditions of their deposits that if the bank goes bankrupt it will compensate the depositors from its own capital. So, why was IBB pushed to do this? It would appear that this was a case of poor analysis and misunderstanding of the situation on the part of the FSA. So, it is very important to understand how to analyse the situation, what type of law and regulations are applicable and how the contract fulfils those obligations.

It is not necessary to make many changes, and much can be achieved using the current system. If the FSA had allowed IBB to pursue its own contract, there would have been no problem. Unfortunately, that did not happen, and now IBB has come up with a new deposit product, based on *wakalah*. It does not mention anything about protection and fulfils all of the *Shari'a* and legal requirements without making any changes. So, it can be done with the correct analysis and if people open their minds about the real situation.

There is a very important issue with regard to regulators and policy makers. That is the question, what is a deposit? It is an important definition, from both a legal and *Shari'a* point-of-view. The regulators are really concerned with the stability of the system as a whole. It is their philosophy that if deposits are not guaranteed, all the depositors will come demanding their money at once, and there will be a 'bank run'. It seems that there is not so much a misunderstanding, but the regulators in the UK have said that 'deposit' has a very specific meaning for them. If you would like to establish a bank, then it must fulfil the requirements of the FSA. One can look also to other types of financial institutions, such as wholesale banking, which has similar complications with regard to regulation, and also mutual funds.

It should be recognised that the situation in Europe is different from that in the Middle East. In the Middle East, certain *Shari'a* aspects can be accommodated, and the bank can 'say' that it will guarantee the depositors against default with its capital, but in the West what is required is regulatory guarantee, and it is not sufficient simply to 'say' what the bank would do in the case of default. It must be written in the contract, and that is totally different. A project, a *murabaha* contract with an early payment rebate, had to be cancelled in the Netherlands for exactly that reason. It is common practice in the West to give a rebate if the customer repays a loan before the full term of the contract, but in Islamic finance this is not acceptable under a *murabaha* contract. This is a new question that has been raised here in the West, and with issues of this type it is necessary that the Islamic finance industry come together, not just at the local level, but at the country level and at the European level, to resolve these issues. Questions regarding *takaful*, insurance regulation on the asset side and deposit guarantee schemes all need to be raised at the European level. It may be time to put these issues on the EU agenda, because there is a limit to what can be achieved at the country level. Some steps have been made, initiated by France and the UK, to centralise this coordination at the European level.

Establishing a bank is a very difficult exercise because of this deposit issue. As it can be resolved, it does not pose a big challenge; however for Islamic banking there are other issues. First is the question of liquidity, which is particularly difficult for Islamic banks because they cannot access the conventional interbank market because of the prohibition of *riba*. There is an Islamic interbank market, and there are ways for these banks to access funds, but the Banque de France is very concerned that in the ultimate scenario, that arises from time to time today, an Islamic bank should be capable of accessing liquidity from the European Central Bank (ECB) directly, which raises the question of the collateral that the Islamic bank could put up as security for that financing. So, liquidity is very important for Islamic banks, and thus it is advisable to have discussions with some major Islamic banks which have dealt with this issue, such as Kuwait Finance House and Qatar Islamic Bank.

Another important point is how accounting affects the prudential treatment of something like *murabaha*, which is sale and re-sale with a deferred price. That form is two different sales, but economically it is a financing operation. How should it be treated from an accounting point of view? IFRS would suggest that substance had precedence over form, so it would be considered financing, which may have some consequences with respect to Basel II and Cook ratios. French GAAP is more concerned with form than substance, so it should be considered as a double sale, which does not have the same cost in terms of equity funds that must be put aside. Banking is a very tricky thing, essential for the economy and systemic, leading to the 'too big to fail dilemma'. It is a difficult exercise, and it is where a partnership must be established with Islamic banks.

In the context of Spain, however, it should be asked whether retail banking is really necessary. Islamic banking is fairly complex, of course, but it is not a given that it is as relevant for Spain as for France, with its large domestic Muslim population, or the UK, which was seeking some social inclusion. So it may be helpful to step back from this complex issue and consider whether there really is a need for retail Islamic banking in Spain in the first place. For example,

Korea wanted to tap into the liquidity available in the Islamic markets, but it was not really interested in the retail market initially. Its interest was to enter the capital market, so it first explored offshore *sukuk* issuance so that companies could access funding. From there, it is possible to evaluate the need to transition from offshore into onshore, and if necessary, into retail Islamic banking.

Spain has a significant Muslim population, much of which has come from Morocco, and hence it is not as large as in France. As it seems to be more recently developed, Spain Muslims are probably less likely to have adapted themselves to Western culture than in France, and they closer to their origins. The example can be cited of a Spanish lawyer of Moroccan origin, who has found that she is unable to avoid using the Spanish banking system. She does have a savings account, and those savings yield interest, so what she does is to give those interest payments to charity, because she does not want to be practising something which is not in line with *Shari'a*. Furthermore, she does not own any property in Spain because there is no bank that will give her the opportunity to finance the purchase of real estate through proper Islamic, *Shari'a*-compliant products. This may be an exception, but it does show that there is at least some interest in that respect.

Spain is not very experienced in Islamic finance. However, it has had occasion to deal with banks in the Islamic world with respect to mega-projects in the region. The main constraint in those contracts has been the wording, substitution of the word 'creditor' for 'the provider of the facility', 'debtor' for 'the user of the facility' and 'interest' for 'the deferred payment charges'. The words are changed, but the concepts remain the same. This is not in relation to an Islamic banking product but a buyer credit facility or another financing of foreign trade. Of course, Islamic finance must be more than just wording, and the situation would be different when specifically using Islamic products. The main objective is to learn which products can be adapted to the Spanish legislation and the adaptation that is needed, big or small, by the Bank of Spain, regulators or government, to implement those products.

It is absolutely necessary that Spanish authorities, regulators and legislators join this effort because otherwise it is not feasible. The difficulty is whether they are ready to do so. Ideally they will be, but they have other problems to address at present, so perhaps the timing of such a project is not ideal, although it would appear to be a time when it is most needed. The French were very wise in starting two years ago so that they are, more or less, ready at this time when Islamic finance is needed. The required changes are going to be part of a long process, and unless there is someone within the administration making an effort to form a committee, as in the French example, and organise a body of experts to look at all the aspects of law and regulation, it will be a tremendous task.

It is conceivable, however, to adapt some of the products that are already in force under Spanish legislation, such as project finance or leasing. One example is that of *murabaha*, which is essentially two subsequent sales. In Spain, that is known simply as *compra venta*, a sale-and-purchase agreement. The issue is to achieve the same goal, which is to provide finance to a company, using two sales and purchases, which has VAT, notaries, registration fees and other considerations. That makes it less attractive, but the underlying concept is still *compra venta*. *Salam* contracts are simply *compra venta a plazos* in the end, the same concepts but sometimes with little adjustments.

In project finance, there is *istisna'a* and *ijarah*. Payment in instalments or when milestones are achieved, which is purely *istisna'a*, is a concept that is no stranger to Spain. *Ijarah* is a lease, which is a bit more complicated, since there is no definition of leasing in Spain, so it is necessary to bring together all the pieces of legislation to do it. One very important thing is that in all leases it is necessary to differentiate between the principal and the interest, which is something that cannot be avoided. *Ijarah*-to-own, a lease contract with a purchase option, is quite straightforward, but certain things must be specified for such an agreement to be tax efficient. To allow the lessee to take advantage of the tax benefit, not only of the amortisation of the asset which the lessee is understood to be acquiring, but also of the financial charge that is embedded, it is necessary that the bank, or the entity conducting the financing as a lessor, specify in the invoices the amount of the interest that is being paid on a monthly basis and the amount of the refund of the principle that is being paid by the lessee. Interest is a matter of wording, but it could be adjusted so as to take advantage of the tax benefits where applicable.

Again, it is a case of form versus substance. In some cases, substance is the relevant point to be examined, while in others it is the form. From an accounting point of view, for example, the issues are different to those from a legal, or from a tax and regulatory point of view. With the introduction of international accounting standards it is much easier to defend that, regardless of form, the transaction is a lease with an option to purchase, or with an intention to purchase on the lessee. Whatever the form being used, accounting-wise, and probably tax-wise also, it should be treated as a lease. However from a formal point of view there is Article 115 of the Spanish Corporate Income Tax Law, that states that the tax authorities want to know the amount that is being paid in interest and how much of the principle is being repaid. That may raise issues with respect to how the *ijarah* is written and should be applied.

With respect to wording, it is possible that some scholars also accept the wording on the conventional side. For example, for leasing in the United States, scholars have accepted that the beneficiary declares interest rather than rent, for tax purposes, in the *Shari'a* leasing contract. This has been accepted because the local regulations are written that way. Perhaps that is an extreme case, but one should always work to adopt the correct forms of Islamic finance and only in very special cases, when there is no alternative, something of this nature might be considered by scholars. The emphasis, however, should be on what can be done, what can be adopted or changed to make sure that Islamic finance is done in the right way.

In some cases, for professionals and Islamic scholars, it may be easier to work from an existing contract from the bank in which a similar transaction was performed. It would be easier to try to change the methodology and the terminology in the contract. However, that is not enough. The process of how the transaction takes place must be changed, and there must be an asset which is involved in the process, being bought, or leased, or similar, in order to ensure that there are deferred payment charges and that it is not purely a loan. There must be an asset which has been allocated. It cannot be just a pure loan with interest payable. It is possible to change an existing contract, making it easy to understand for the bank and the credit committee and the lawyers; however, that is not changing very much, just terminology, and it is the process itself that must change. The processes of buying, selling or leasing an underlying asset are ways to make sure that the contract has changed.

Changing terminology means changing obligation. That is very important. It is not purely changing 'interest' to 'rent'; from a legal point of view, it is now a lease contract, and there is now an asset involved. The client has become a lessee and is paying rent, which is not a minor change, but rather a change in the obligation in the contract. If that contract is a conventional lease contract, and everything around it has been adapted from a conventional lease, that is fine, as long as the obligation is understood and it is agreed on what basis the payments are being made. If those payments are designated with reference to some base rate or interest rate, as with a conventional debt, that is irrelevant as long as it is clear that the payment is rent and that is acceptable from a *Shari'a* point of view.

There is a project in France to issue *sukuk* based on a real estate portfolio which was initially leased conventionally. An audit of that portfolio revealed that 10 to 15 per cent of the initial leasing agreements were not *Shari'a* compliant. That is to say that the remainder, the vast majority, posed no particular issue. So, it is not a big story to have a leasing agreement issued today by a conventional bank which is *Shari'a* compliant. There are some philosophical aspects, such as that in an *ijarah* agreement in which the lessor should really be considered the owner of the building and not merely an agent acquiring the asset on behalf of the lessees. Once that is understood, there are some legal consequences in terms of what happens in the case of expropriation. In a conventional lease, the lessee will usually indemnify the lessor for any loss, whereas if the lessor is the owner, then he ought to be the party to bear that risk. It is similar in terms of insurance. If the building were destroyed completely and there were a shortfall in the amount of insurance cover provided, in a conventional lease that would be borne by the lessee, but according to the *Shari'a* point of view, the owner should bear that risk. It is not such a painful exercise; it is realistic, and the message to take away is that Islamic finance-style transactions are being implemented without conscious realisation. It requires some adjustment, not pure wording and not form over substance, which tends to be a caricature of Islamic finance.

One question worth considering in this interim period, until the Spanish regulations are updated to comply with Islamic finance requirements, is whether it would be worthwhile to move certain assets to other European jurisdictions, for example, the UK or France, to attract Islamic investors by using forms that are more familiar for them. In particular, it would be useful to know whether, in order to avoid transfer taxes, which seems to be one of the main obstacles, it would be possible to construct a kind of synthetic transaction by which the equity portion of the financing would be moved into a British- or French-based vehicle and for that vehicle to issue some sort of bond, a *sukuk*, that could then be sold to Islamic investors. This could be used to accelerate the process of Spanish enterprises taking advantage of Islamic finance, because the possibility of implementing Islamic finance entirely in Spain could be a long-term proposition.

It could be an attractive proposition if there are assets that can be moved to the UK, even if that were done on a conventional basis and transferred into a UK-based special purpose vehicle (SPV), which would then hold the asset. Even if that transaction were done conventionally, as long as the SPV in the UK was actually holding the asset, the *sukuk* could be issued to finance that vehicle or asset.

Anglo-Saxon jurisdictions, such as England and the US, seem to be better suited – more pre-adapted – to meet the requirements of *Shari'a*-compliant products, and there are at least two reasons for this. First is the concept of trust, which is very useful in this type of scheme, and the second is the idea of beneficial ownership versus economic ownership. Those two factors are very relevant, especially in the issuance of *sukuk* and in establishing the link between the asset and the ownership of it by the *sukuk* holders. Civil law jurisdictions are more formal and do not allow for this double concept of economic and legal ownership. In that respect, even once all the required amendments are introduced in Spanish courts and Spanish law, England, as an Anglo-Saxon jurisdiction, will still be more flexible than Spain.

It is very interesting to know that with assets that are movable, for instance aircraft, vessels or any other means of transport, it could be possible to use them in UK-based structures. However, if there are no movable assets, for instance, real estate assets, electrical grids, railways and these sorts of assets which are interesting in terms of Islamic finance, even if a UK trust is being used to issue the *sukuk*, the real estate, for example, is still based in Spain, and this means that one must still deal with the Spanish registry. Perhaps it is an extreme example, but it is not clear how the co-ownership of the *sukuk* holders could be registered with respect to Spanish real estate. How would Spanish property rights recognise that there is an indirect legal ownership, to the extent that it is required under *Shari'a* principles to make the structure feasible? Part of the problem can be detached, but in certain transactions the Spanish legal issues still must be addressed, and that is why adaptation or interpretation of the regulations is needed to make that possible.

In the case of immovable assets, it would still be possible to transfer them to an SPV in the UK, and the ownership and registration in Spain, for example, would simply be in the name of the SPV. It is actually the company in the UK issuing the *sukuk* for the assets in Spain. That is something that should be possible as long as the *sukuk* holders really own the company, the SPV, that owns the asset. This can be the structure, without going into complex registrations in Spain. That may be problematic in some transactions, for example, those related to energy project finance, because the collateral is the rights attached to certain administrative rights.

It is not the case that *sukuk* can be done only when the asset is physically transferred. It is still possible, for instance, in the case of thermo-solar plants, other energy products, or any asset that cannot be transferred. There is a lease agreement which can be securitised, and the *sukuk* can be issued on the lease agreement. For example, if a railway company wants to issue *sukuk*, then it can set up a company and lease the railway asset to that company, and then that company will issue the *sukuk*. The only potential complication may be if there is stamp duty payable on the long-term lease agreement; this is, however, usually a minor cost which must be incurred, and there are different structures that can work on this.

Strategic securitisation, which avoids an actual transfer of the asset, is not useful in this situation either, since Islamic finance is based on tangible assets, and therefore the assets would need to be transferred. Transferring only the risk, but not the ownership, is completely non-*Shari'a* compliant, and strategic securitisation, in terms of credit default swaps and such instruments, is of no benefit.

However, wholesale securitisation may be an option in Europe. In the example of the East Cameron Partners *sukuk*, they had two SPVs, one based in the United States, where the limited liability company was actually acquiring participatory interest in East Cameron Partners, based in Louisiana, and another, off-shore vehicle which issued the *sukuk* and funded the SPV in Delaware to actually buy that participatory interest. So, it need not be just tangible assets like properties which would incur transfer tax, and there is also participatory interest, *musharaka* partnership. Capital is contributed to the business being funded, which is another option that can be explored.

There was one securitisation deal in Saudi Arabia where the asset was a fleet of vehicles and the rents were passed and financed by investors who were also the owners of the cars. Since in Saudi Arabia assets can be owned only by Saudi residents, two SPVs were set up; one in Saudi Arabia which owned the car fleet and another, which was funded by an SPV in Ireland, that was issuing the *sukuk*. Apparently, this is acceptable, and a *fatwa* was issued by serious scholars, so that may well be a way to do what might be called, from an economic point of view, 'strategic securitisation'. The assets could be maintained in Spain, for example, and funding would come through a trust vehicle in Ireland or the UK, which could be a good compromise to do this business Islamically without waiting for everything to change.

In terms of mortgages, there are different types of Islamic mortgage, structured in different ways. Usually, the interest payment from the client will be in the form of rent as part of a lease agreement, and there will be some kind of partnership between the bank and the client to purchase the assets. The most popular and flexible is called a 'diminishing *musharaka* and *ijarah*' contract. In a conventional mortgage, the client will pay a percentage of the purchase price as a deposit, and the bank will finance the remaining portion. The client will then repay the capital to the bank, with interest, over the term of the mortgage. In the Islamic mortgage, with the Islamic terminology, there is a partnership agreement, *musharaka*, where the client will pay a percentage of the purchase price, like the conventional deposit, and the bank will pay the remaining part. Each party then owns a part of the property according to the proportion they have contributed to the purchase price. The client then occupies the property under a lease contract, *ijarah*, which is arranged so that, over time, the client, as well as paying rent, will purchase from the bank their share of the property. Hence, the diminishing aspect of the *musharaka* as the ownership is gradually transferred. The rental payments constitute, in part, the bank's return on the asset and, in part, a repayment of the capital contributed by the bank in the initial purchase.

In Spain, it is analogous to *comunidad de bienes*, where the bank and the borrower jointly own the real estate asset, and then the *communidad* leases the asset to the client, that is, to the borrower. Then the borrower pays rent, which remunerates both parties, but on one side it is remuneration for the bank as the owner, and on the other side, the borrower's side, it is being used to purchase the interest that the bank has in the co-ownership of the asset.

In England, there is a contract called 'shared ownership' which is very well practised in housing associations. It is designed for those who have less income and limited means as a way to assist them in owning their own properties. It is, again, another example of the practice of Islamic finance without using the name. Around the time that Islamic finance was introduced in England in 1997, a comparison was made of the shared ownership contract and *ijarah-murabaha*. In that case, shared ownership seemed to be preferable for being very equitable and practical. With an Islamic mortgage, one may be tied into the contract until the end of its 25-year term; however, in shared ownership, it is possible to exit, or complete, at any time. It is possible to exercise a claim over the part that the bank owns, just as it is possible to terminate the contract and realise the capital gains. This is not the case with Islamic mortgages.

The experience of Scotland was quite interesting, the law there being different to that of England regarding leasing contracts. In Scotland, the maximum term of a lease is just seven years, which does not suffice for the purpose of Islamic mortgages, since the normal term would be 20 to 25 years. The solution was to take away the leasing contract and replace it with an occupancy contract. This was only changing the terminology, not only to accommodate the Islamic banking principles but also to work within the Scottish law. The remuneration paid was, therefore, for occupancy, and so there was no more rent, and the contract avoided the legislation prohibiting a term of greater than seven years. This type of arrangement, again, in substance was a leasing agreement, but in form was something different, yet remained fully *Shari'a* compliant. It shows that it is possible to work around the existing legislation by using different forms and still be compatible with Islamic principles.

It is interesting to note from this example that simply because something is not covered by the existing legislation it does not mean that it cannot be done. Spain, like France, has the principle of the freedom to contract, which basically maintains that parties can agree upon certain terms, provided that this agreement is not intended to circumvent rules of public order and that the agreement will benefit from the proper tax treatment. There are some caveats, but it is true to say that, as with the Scottish example, if the lease agreement does not serve the purposes of the parties involved because of the seven-year restriction, as long as the alternative occupancy agreement does not violate Scottish rules of public order and provides rents which are tax deductible for the lessee, that is fine. This is where it is really possible to approach Islamic finance completely open-mindedly and not be concerned about differing legislation. In principle, the legislation is not required, but more tax clarification and interpretations are.

The reality is that the current system, as a whole, is biased towards debt contracts, which is something that needs to be rebalanced as far as Islamic finance is concerned. If it is possible to push a little further and begin to give people more choice with respect to using equity, as opposed to debt, to finance their properties, there will be fewer sub-prime and related problems. That will require thinking about the tax implications of Islamic finance and which of the variety of Islamic contracts available will be the best way to do it.

In France, there is a definition of credit operation that is very *Shari'a* friendly. It is very basic and does not use the term 'interest'. There are four kinds of operation: loans, leasing, receivable mobilisation and banking guarantee. The definition is very broad, and within the legal framework of France this general framework can be used for all kinds of credit operations. Sometimes there are some obstacles with respect to diminishing *musharaka* and *ijarah*, as there is really no rule in order to have legal security. That is why France will need to rethink this instrument, and it could be more important than *murabaha*. *Murabaha* has a lot of critics who say that it is not really *Shari'a* compliant and the proposition of the IFSB or the IDB concerning the stability of the financial system was that this instrument be the new way for credit operations.

Many similarities can be found between conventional and Islamic finance, and the reason for this could be that in Islamic finance most of the products available have been reverse-engineered to replicate the conventional instruments. What happens is that the concept of interest gets embedded into credit sales. That is why the similarities are so profound. Regardless of whether one talks about interest, rent or mark-up, the distinction has come down to whether an asset is involved or not. As long as there is an asset, it can be made to fit with *Shari'a*. It could be possible to replace debt with equity in some of the contracts, for instance, in the example of shared-ownership home financing, and looking at Islamic finance from that perspective, the differences and the advantages emerge. Much of the confusion is really born of semantics, because of an interest in making finance take the form of trading or leasing. It may be trading or leasing in form, but it is finance with embedded interest in substance, and once that issue is cleared up in everyone's mind it will become easier to address the tax issues and other things.

Co-operative banking is a very interesting form of banking that may have examples to learn from. Although they do exist in Spain, they are largely limited to the agricultural sector, and even there they are not commonplace. In France, it is known as *Banque Mutuel* or *Cooperative*, but it refers more to the way that these saving banks operate internally and the way they share the profits with customers, who are at the same time the shareholders of the bank. That is the mutual aspect. Otherwise, they practise a conventional banking business: although they share the profits, these profits are generated in a completely non-*Shari'a*-compliant manner. Hence in Spain the co-operative banks are under the supervision of the Bank of Spain and can pursue any banking transactions, the difference being just in how their profits are allocated. Probably, in the beginning it was similar to a *Shari'a*-compliant institution, but it has evolved and has had to be regulated; in the end the result resembles more a conventional bank than a mutual institution.

One big financial question related to Islamic finance is that of returns. It is clear that an Islamic investor is investing in equity, and in the world of conventional finance, equity investors are looking for very high returns, while debt investors require a much lower yield. This raises the question of the returns that an Islamic investor will expect in the case of performing a form of equity transaction. If the Islamic investor is seeking the typical 20 per cent return for equity while interest rates are just 5 per cent, then the numbers will not work.

For infrastructure projects, there will be a very decent return through Build Operate Transfer (BOT) financing, and it will be perfectly Islamic. Furthermore, those respectable returns are quite secure, since people will use the train, the roads and other such modes, and it is not likely that people will suddenly stop using those services. So, it is high-return, low-risk, perfectly Islamic and, therefore, well suited to this kind of equity investment.

Another experience in the UK has been around the issue of VAT. When IBB started, there was a problem of how a bank could acquire goods and re-sell them to customers without the multiplication in VAT, since that would impact upon the margin that the bank is like to receive. The response from the British tax office was that it would be very difficult to remedy as it was a European-level law, which would require recourse to Brussels. The process dragged on for a year and a half until, eventually, a new person at the tax office looked at the case and identified a clause which states that, in terms of banking, if the remuneration or payment that the bank is receiving is a result of a deferred payment, then VAT is not applicable. All that was required was that a VAT instruction be issued explaining that the income received is therefore the deferred payment of a sale, falls under that legislation and is VAT exempt. After a year and a half, no change was actually required – it was just a case of the authorities opening their minds to the real nature of the situation with respect to the income the bank is receiving, which is very similar to what a conventional bank receives. It is another example of how often changes are not really required, just clarifications of the existing rules and legislation.

The same situation exists in France with respect to *murabaha* and the exoneration of VAT, resulting from European case law. A deferred payment is, after all, a credit operation, and hence there is exoneration on VAT. VAT is a very interesting subject because the norms within all 27 EU member states are based on the same VAT directive and based on the same law, but it is often interpreted differently, not only in its transcription into the laws of the member states but also in its application in those states. In these cases, the deferred payment is really an interest charge, which makes perfect sense if the payment is being made to a bank, since banks are accustomed to receiving deferred payments and charging interest on that basis. However, from a formal point of view, it also has the nature of a sale; so there is the conflict between substance and form once again.

The Netherlands is very good at resolving this type of conflict. It always looks at the substance of the agreement and is very amenable to overlooking the format, especially with respect to financial transactions. It is very interested in identifying interest, regardless of whether embedded in rent, the purchase price or in any other form. The typical case in Spain, however, is more difficult. Considering securitisation deals in France, Spain, Italy, the Netherlands and the UK, it is easy to see that the advice given with respect to VAT is different in each case, because each tax authority has its own interpretation, even though they are all working from the same EU directive. This is especially true with respect to financial products and services. Some jurisdictions, for instance, the Dutch, will be more practical, which in legal terms would mean giving preference to substance of form. Others will be more formal in their approach; for example, Spain looking at the leasing agreement and the deferred payment, which would be treated as a sale, and incur VAT. Ideally, the experiences of the UK and the Netherlands can be drawn upon, when approaching the Spanish tax office, to show that there is a precedent for that kind of treatment. So, there are conflicts that arise, even across the EU when applying the same VAT directive. There ought to be one set of rules that are the same for everyone, but in practice that is, unfortunately, not the case.

Islamic insurance is usually done through an instrument known as *takaful*. There are many challenges surrounding this instrument since, in principle, *takaful* is a mutual structure, and the laws have changed significantly so as to discourage mutual structures – so much so that mutual organisations have been de-mutualising. It is, therefore, very difficult to have a shared pool, unsupported by a third party, where *takaful* participants can manage their risk.

There is a view forming that is reasonably close to the Islamic alternative, but there are differences. For instance, in *takaful*, the participants, rather than paying a premium, actually make a conditional donation. It is conditional that the participants actually receive a benefit from the protection provided by the pool. That is a difficult concept. Once the pool has been established, if all the participants lodge claims against the pool, which cannot actually be met, there is a problem of solvency. That is a severe problem that has led to the creation of hybrid structures, involving a mutual fund and a shareholding company. If the pool is in deficit, the *takaful* operator will actually provide a so-called non-interest-bearing loan to the *takaful* pool to manage those claims. This raises a lot of prudential and legal issues, and possibly more problems than are seen on the 'equity versus debt' side of Islamic finance. Islamic insurance is still something of a work in progress.

A *takaful* company that ran in Europe for over ten years, based in Luxembourg, did not experience problems associated so much with the structure. A limited company, working on a *mudaraba* structure for the *takaful*, it did not experience regulation problems as far as the *takaful* was concerned. The main problem concerned the investment of the premiums, or donations. That was due to the third European directive from 1995, and now it is even more complicated due to the asset classes that must be respected in the terms of investment. Working with a *mudaraba* model, or even a *wakalah* model, should be within both local and European regulations, and the *mudaraba* model practised in Luxembourg never presented any problems because of that.

There was one *takaful* company, based in the UK, Salaam Insurance, which was forced to close because of the business itself and the lack of granularity of the portfolio. Salaam Insurance, underwritten by Principle Insurance, was the first *takaful* company to be authorised by a financial services agency in the Western world. There were some regulatory complications initially, but the FSA in the UK had learned a lot about Islamic finance before this came around, and the issues were eventually resolved, and there was nothing with which the company could not comply from a regulatory point of view. There were some challenges associated with re-insurance, or re-*takaful*, because it was not available at the time, especially with the unlimited payment compensation that exists for car insurance in the UK. As the existing re-*takaful* companies had difficulty in complying with that, the scholar approved a combination of conventional reinsurance and re-*takaful*, on the proviso that if the full re-*takaful* capability becomes available then the company would have to move completely to re-*takaful*.

The problem the company had was a question of pricing the premium, or 'contribution', as it was called in the documentation. The conventional insurance model in the UK is 'postcode pricing', where premiums are largely determined by the area in which the client lives. Unfortunately, this type of model penalises much of the Muslim population of the UK. The advice given to the management at the time was that adopting such a model would lead them to pricing themselves out of the market. However, that was how they proceeded, which resulted in a pricing three times that of conventional insurance premiums. They continued like that for six months, but the business model they had adopted was not successful. There is a chance that they will return to the market, having consolidated their capital and revised their business model.

To conclude, consider again the last of the ten questions proposed at the beginning. Supposing that the Spanish government were to form a committee to explore the introduction of Islamic finance, what would be the road map for that process? The situation in France has provided some good examples and some good advice. In fact, the preliminary step of government of establishing that committee would fit with that example, recognising the potential of Islamic economics and finance. The initial steps, after forming the committee, would be to audit the current legislative and regulatory environment to identify potential barriers. In the early stage, it is recommended to avoid new legislation wherever possible. It is also important at this stage to translate some of the material that is available, especially as far as standards are concerned. It is important to have standardised products that are very clear to the regulators. The AAOIFI standards are one suggestion, but the IFSB and some other institutions also produce valuable material. There are *Shari'a* consultancies available, and scholars who can provide the service themselves, but other institutions, such the Islamic Fiqh Academy at the IOC, may also be able to provide guidance. A broad base of opinion is advisable. Liquidity management is an important issue that needs to be addressed, and the Malaysian experiments in this area could provide some interesting feedback.

These are the main issues for the road map for introducing Islamic finance, but it is important to recognise that it will be a gradual process, and it is not possible to have it all at once. Therefore, it is advisable to start with the most simple products and institutions, those that can be established with the least amount of new regulation or adjustment, and then build on that to integrate the others.

It certainly is a case of having to go back to the roots, to the simplest forms. Those principles and contracts are embedded in the Spanish civil code and, to some extent, in Spanish tax laws. The issue of uncertainty, which is very relevant from a legal point of view, will require either adaptation of interpretation of the existing regulations, but without the introduction of new contracts, or new forms that would only make things more difficult. Tax issues are extremely relevant because tax legislation is based on the distinction between equity and debt, whereas under Islamic finance principles there is only equity, and therefore a large adjustment in the analysis will be required. For corporations, there is an incentive to create debt, since it generates tax-deductible interest; therefore it is important that the payments made under the different Islamic finance instruments also be tax deductible to ensure their efficiency. The collaboration of many institutions is certainly required, starting with the government, legislators, scholars, academics, the legal profession and, finally, the consumers, clients and companies. The key is in adapting Islamic finance to the needs of Spanish clients and consumers while also adapting the market to serve the needs of Islamic financiers.

Each country has had its own reasons for pursuing Islamic finance. Korea, for instance, was pursuing the capital markets in order to access liquidity. The UK really wanted to see retail banking to foster some sort of social inclusion. That is something that has not been seen in France just yet, and it may be a while before Spain is ready for such a move. However, instead of waiting for the government, a group should be established to lobby for the changes necessary. In the UK, it took ten years to reach the stage that they began to treat the legislation. The French top-down approach has been slightly different, being government led, possibly in response to the crisis. The Koreans started specifically with *sukuk* for gaining capital investment, which might be a sensible approach for Spain.

It would seem that there are a many parties surrounding this issue of Islamic finance, all of whom are interested in seeing its introduction, so the important step is to form that group to pressure the government, to demonstrate the demand for those services and that Islamic finance is a reality. These efforts would also benefit greatly from being coordinated at the EU level, drawing on the experience of the UK and France. Ideally, this can be achieved without the need to wait, in Spain as in the UK, another ten years to see Islamic finance embraced as a reality.

Part II
Additional Articles

5
The Global Financial Crisis: Can Islamic Finance Help?

M. Umer Chapra

The whole world is now in the grip of a financial crisis which is far more serious than any experienced since the Great Depression. It has taken more than $3 trillion of bailout and liquidity injections by a number of industrial countries to abate somewhat the intensity of the crisis. Nevertheless, there are fears that this crisis may have exposed the world economy to a long period of economic slowdown. There is, hence, a call for a new architecture that would help minimise the frequency and severity of such crises in the future.

Primary cause of the crisis

It is not possible to design a new architecture without first determining the primary cause of the all the crises. The generally recognised most important cause of almost all crises has been excessive and imprudent lending by banks over a long period. This is clearly acknowledged by the Bank for International Settlements (BIS), which states as much in its annual report (released on 30th June 2008).

This raises the question of what makes it possible for banks to resort to such an unhealthy practice which not only destabilises the financial system but is also not in their own interest in the long run. There are three factors that make this possible. First is inadequate market discipline in the financial system, resulting from the absence of profit-and-loss sharing (PLS). The second is the mind-boggling expansion in the size of derivatives, particularly credit default swaps (CDSs); and the third is the 'too big to fail' concept, which tends to give an assurance to big banks that the central bank will definitely come to their rescue and not allow them to fail.

The false sense of immunity from losses that all of these factors together has introduced a fault line in the financial system. Banks have not, therefore, undertaken a careful evaluation of their loan applications. This has led to an unhealthy expansion in the overall volume of credit, to excessive leverage, and to an unsustainable rise in asset prices, living beyond means and speculative investment. Unwinding later on gives rise to a steep decline in asset prices and to financial frangibility and debt crises, particularly if there is over-indulgence in short sales. Jean Claude Trichet, president of the European Central Bank, has rightly pointed out that 'a bubble is more likely to develop when investors can leverage their positions by investing borrowed funds'.

The sub-prime mortgage crisis

The sub-prime mortgage crisis, in the grip of which the US finds itself at present, is a classical example of excessive and imprudent lending. Securitisation or the 'originate-to-distribute' model of financing has played a crucial role in this. The creation of collateral-ised debt obligations (CDOs) by mixing prime and sub-prime debt made it possible for mortgage originators to pass the entire risk of default of even sub-prime debt to the ultimate purchasers who would have normally been reluctant to bear such a risk.

Mortgage originators had, therefore, less incentive to undertake careful underwriting.

Consequently, loan volume gained greater priority over loan quality and the amount of lending to sub-prime borrowers and speculators increased steeply. According to Ben Bernanke, chair-man of the Board of Governors of the US Federal Reserve System, 'Far too much of the lending in recent years was neither responsible nor prudent. In addition, abusive, unfair, or deceptive lending prac-tices led some borrowers into mortgages that they would not have chosen knowingly.' The check that market discipline could have exercised on self-interest did not come into play. Even the supervi-sors failed to perform their task effectively by not taking serious notice of the unfair practices at an early stage and nipping them in the bud.

The result is that a number of banks either have failed or have had to be bailed out or nationalised by the governments in the US, the UK, Europe and a number of other places. This has created uncertainty in the market and prolonged the credit crunch, which made it hard for even healthy banks to find financing. There is a lurking fear that this might be only the tip of the iceberg and that a lot more may follow if the crisis causes a prolonged recession and leads to defaults on the part of credit card institutions, corporations and derivatives dealers.

When there is immoderate and imprudent lending, and lenders are not confident of repayment, there is an excessive resort to derivatives like CDSs to seek protection against default. The buyer of the swap (creditor) pays a premium to the seller (a hedge fund) for the compensation he will receive in case the debtor defaults. If this protection had been confined to the actual creditor, there might not have been any problem. What happened, however, was that hedge funds sold the swaps not to just the actual lending bank but also to a large number of others who were willing to bet on the default of the debtor. These swap holders, in turn, resold the swaps to others. The whole process continued several times.

While a genuine insurance contract indemnifies only the actually insured party, in the case of CDSs there were several swap holders who had to be compensated. This accentuated the risk and made it difficult for the hedge funds and banks to honour their commitments. The notional amount of all outstanding derivatives (including CDSs of $54.6 trillion) is currently estimated by the BIS to be over $600 trillion, more than ten times the size of the world economy. No wonder George Soros described derivatives as 'hydrogen bombs', and Warren Buffett called them 'financial weapons of mass destruction'.

The Islamic financial system

One of the most important objectives of Islam is to realise greater justice in human society. According to the *Qur'an*, a society where there is no justice will ultimately head towards decline and destruction (*Qur'an*, 57:25). Justice requires a set of rules or moral values, which everyone accepts and faithfully complies with. The financial system may be able to promote justice if, in addition to being strong and stable, it satisfies at least two conditions based on moral values. One of these is that the financier should also share in the risk so as not to shift the entire burden of losses to the entrepreneur, and the other is that an equitable share of financial resources mobilised by financial institutions should become available to the poor to help eliminate poverty, expand employment and self-employment opportunities and, thus, help reduce inequalities of income and wealth.

To fulfil the first condition of justice, Islam requires both the financier and the entrepreneur to equitably share the profit as well as the loss. For this purpose, one of the basic principles of Islamic finance is 'No risk, no gain'. This should help introduce greater discipline into the financial system by motivating financial institutions to assess the risks more carefully and to effectively monitor the use of funds by the borrowers. The double assessment of risks by both the financier and the entrepreneur should help inject greater discipline into the system and go a long way toward reducing excessive lending.

Islamic finance should, in its ideal form, help raise substantially the share of equity and PLS in businesses. Greater reliance on equity financing has supporters even in mainstream economics. Professor Kenneth Rogoff of Harvard University states that in an ideal world, equity lending and direct investment would play a much bigger role.

Greater reliance on equity does not necessarily mean that debt financing is ruled out. This is because all the financial needs of individuals, firms or governments cannot be made amenable to equity and PLS. Debt is, therefore, indispensable but should not be promoted for non-essential and wasteful consumption and unproductive speculation. For this purpose, the Islamic financial system does not allow the creation of debt through direct lending and borrowing. It rather requires the creation of debt through the sale or lease of real assets by means of its sales- and lease-based modes of financing (*murabaha, ijarah, salam, istisna'a* and *sukuk*). The purpose is to enable an individual or firm to buy the urgently needed real goods and services in conformity with his or her ability to make the payment later. It has, however, laid down a number of conditions, some of which are:

- The asset which is being sold or leased must be real, and not imaginary or notional.
- The seller or lessor must own and possess the goods being sold or leased.
- The transaction must be a genuine trade transaction with full intention of giving and taking delivery.

- The debt cannot be sold, and thus the risk associated with it must be borne by the lender himself.

The first condition will help eliminate a large number of derivatives transactions which involve nothing more than gambling by third parties who aspire to claim compensation for losses which have been actually suffered only by the principal party and not by them. The second condition will help ensure that the seller (or lessor) also shares a part of the risk to be able to get a share in the return. Once the seller (financier) acquires ownership and possession of the goods for sale or lease, he or she bears the risk. This condition also puts a constraint on short sales, thereby removing the possibility of a steep decline in asset prices during a downturn. The *Shari'a* has, however, made an exception to this rule in the case of *salam* and *istisna'a,* where the goods are not already available in the market and need to be produced or manufactured before delivery. Financing extended through the Islamic modes can thus expand only in step with the rise of the real economy and thereby help curb excessive credit expansion.

The third and the fourth conditions will not only motivate the creditor to be more cautious in evaluating the credit risk but also prevent an unnecessary explosion in the volume and value of transactions. This will prevent the debt from rising far above the size of the real economy and also release a substantial volume of financial resources for the real sector, thereby helping to expand employment and self-employment opportunities and the production of need-fulfilling goods and services. The discipline that Islam wishes to introduce in the financial system may not, however, materialise unless governments reduce their borrowing from the central bank to a level that is in harmony with the goal of price and financial stability.

One may raise an objection here that all of these conditions will perhaps end up shrinking the size of the economy by reducing the number and volume of transactions. This is not likely to happen, because a number of the speculative and derivatives transactions are generally known to be zero-sum games and have rarely contributed positively to total real output. Hence, a decline in them is also not likely to hurt the real economy.

While a restriction on such transactions will cut the commissions earned by the speculators during an artificially generated boom, it will help them avert losses and bankruptcy that become unavoidable during the decline and lead to a financial crisis. The injection of a greater discipline into the financial system may tend to deprive the sub-prime borrowers of access to credit. Therefore, justice demands that some suitable innovation be introduced in the system to ensure that even small borrowers can get adequate credit. Such borrowers are generally considered to be sub-prime, and their inability to get credit will prevent them from realising their dream of owning homes and establishing their own microenterprises.

There is no doubt that a number of countries have established special institutions to grant credit to the poor and lower-middle-class entrepreneurs. Even though these have been extremely useful, there are two major problems that need to be resolved. One of these is the high cost of finance, ranging from 30 to 84 per cent in the interest-oriented microfinance system. This causes serious hardship to the borrowers in servicing their debt. No wonder the minister of finance for Bangladesh described microcredit interest rates in that country as extortionate in an address he delivered at a microcredit summit in Dhaka in 2004. It is, therefore, important that microcredit be provided to the very poor on a humane, interest-free basis (*qard hasan*). This may be possible if the microfinance system is integrated with *zakat* and *waqf* institutions. For those who can afford to bear the cost of microfinance, it would be better to popularise the Islamic modes of PLS and sales- and lease-based modes of finance, not only to avoid interest but also to prevent the misuse of credit for personal consumption.

Another problem faced by microfinance is that the resources at the disposal of microfinance institutions are inadequate. This problem may be difficult to solve unless the microfinance sector is scaled up by integrating it with the commercial banks. Commercial banks do not generally lend to small borrowers, because of the higher risk and expense involved in such financing. It is, therefore, important to reduce their risk and expense. This may be done partly by a subsidy from *zakat* and *waqf* funds for those borrowers who are eligible for *zakat*.

Thus, we can see that the Islamic financial system is capable of minimising the severity and frequency of financial crises by getting rid of the major weaknesses of the conventional system. It introduces greater discipline into the financial system by requiring the financier to share in the risk. It links credit expansion to the growth of the real economy by allowing credit primarily for the purchase of real goods and services which the seller owns and possesses, and the buyer wishes to receive. It also requires the creditor to bear the risk of default by prohibiting the sale of debt, thereby ensuring that he evaluates the risk more carefully. In addition, Islamic finance can also reduce the problem of sub-prime borrowers by providing credit to them at affordable terms. This will save the billions that are spent after the crisis to bail out the rich bankers. These do not, however, help the poor, because their home may have already become subject to foreclosure and auctioned at a give-away price.

The problem is that the Islamic finance is still in its infancy and shares a very small proportion of international finance. In addition, it does not genuinely reflect the ethos of Islamic teachings. The use of equity and PLS is still very minimal, while that of debt-creating modes is preponderant. Moreover, even in the case of debt-creating modes, all the conditions laid down by the *Shari'a* are not being faithfully observed by the use of legal stratagems (*hiyal*). This is partly due to a lack of proper understanding of the ultimate objectives of Islamic finance, the non-availability of trained personnel, and the absence of a number of shared or support institutions that are needed to minimise the risks associated with anonymity, moral hazard, principal/agent conflict of interest and late settlement of financial obligations. The system is, thus, not fully prepared at present to play a significant role in ensuring the health and stability of the international financial system. It is, however, expected that the system will gradually gain momentum with the passage of time and complement the efforts now being made internationally to promote the health and stability of the global financial system.

Since the current architecture of the conventional financial system has existed for a long time, it may be too much to expect the international community to undertake a radical structural reform of the kind that the Islamic financial system envisages. However, the adoption of some of the elements of the Islamic system, which are also a part of the Western heritage, is indispensable for ensuring the health and stability of the global financial system. These are:

- The proportion of equity in total financing needs to be increased, and that of debt reduced.
- Credit needs to be confined primarily to transactions that are related to the real sector so as to ensure that credit expansion

moves more or less in step with the growth of the real economy and does not promote destabilising speculation and gambling.

- Leverage needs to be controlled to ensure that credit does not exceed the ability of the borrower to repay.
- If the debt instruments, and in particular CDOs, are to be sold, then there should be full transparency about their quality so that the purchaser knows exactly what he is getting into. It would also be desirable to have the right of recourse for the ultimate purchaser of the CDOs to ensure that the lender has an incentive to underwrite the debt carefully.
- While there may be no harm in the use of CDSs to provide protection to the lender against default, it needs to be ensured that the swaps do not become instruments for wagering. Their protective role should be confined to the original lender only and should not cover the other purchasers of swaps who wish to wager on the debtor's default. For this purpose, the derivatives market needs to be properly regulated to remove the element of gambling in it.
- All financial institutions, and not just the commercial banks, need to be properly regulated and supervised so that they remain healthy and do not become a source of systemic risk.
- Some arrangement needs to be made to make credit available to sub-prime borrowers on affordable terms to enable them to buy a home and to establish their own microenterprises. This will help save the financial system from crises resulting from widespread defaults by such borrowers.

6
Points to Ponder in Islamic Finance

Mohamed Ali Elgari

Islamic financial products best fit for infrastructure projects

Due to its participatory nature, Islamic finance lends itself very nicely to infrastructure finance, especially within the private–public partnership (PPP) approach. Infrastructure finance, whenever the private sector is involved, comes under what is called a 'project finance' process. The project itself must generate sufficient income to pay back the project cost and profits to the financiers of the project. This rarely happens without public support. Hence, private–public partnership becomes pivotal.

Such a PPP program is not new to Islamic finance. For hundreds of years, BOT was the predominant scheme of building and rebuilding Awqaf properties.

Many infrastructure projects have been successfully financed on the basis of Islamic finance.

One of the well-known structures is one that consists of *istisna'a*[1] and forward *ijarah*.[2] Private financiers may establish a special purpose vehicle (SPV) that will enter into a forward *ijarah* contract with the public entity which will eventually own the project, through sale. From a *Shari'a* perspective, the subject of this contract is the usufruct of, say, a road or a bridge. The lessee will start making payments immediately after entering into the said contract. The SPV will also enter into procurement contracts with specialised contractors for the construction of the project.

After completion, the project will be delivered to the SPV that is the owner of these assets. The public entity as lessee will use the asset and pay rentals. At the end of the lease term, the asset will be sold or gifted to that public entity.

A project finance structure for green energy

Energy projects are usually quite sizeable and because of this nature, corporate finance may not be capable of supporting them. They are usually structured as project finance. Conventionally, project finance is one form of lending where earnings are just part of the security. In Islamic finance, a project finance structure is based principally on *istisna'a* and a forward lease. It works as follows:

- A project company is established as an SPV through which funds from financiers will go.
- The project company will enter into a procurement contract, usually with the obligor, to build the power-generating station.
- Another contract is signed with the obligor, this time a forward lease whereby the usufruct of the power station is sold for, say, 20 years at a variable rate.
- The obligor starts making the payment immediately after signing the forward lease contract.

Benefitting from Spain's experience

Spain today stands tall in the development of green energy alternatives. Being ahead of most other countries means it has a lot to give to the rest of the world in terms of knowledge and experience. Electricity demand in the Gulf States is growing by three times the world average. It is estimated that no less than $200 billion will be invested in the energy sector in the next few years. Among the GCC members, Saudi Arabia has allocated more than $110 billion for this program, as reported by the media, to produce 2000 megawatts of electricity each year for the next ten years.

The bulk of the new power plants are most probably going to be fuelled by natural gas. However, the government of Saudi Arabia is keen to develop alternative energy sources. KAUST, the internationally acclaimed new university, is building a solar plant as part of a program focusing on clean energy research and development. It is most interesting to know that Saudi Arabia, so far, is not considering nuclear power as an alternative to fossil fuel-based power generation, unlike other Gulf States.

Spain can play a vital role in this respect. However, this role will be defined by Spain's ability to present total solution programs which are not limited to the technical part of a green energy projects but also include the financial segment. It goes without saying that this will include a feasible program of public–private partnership based on *Shari'a*-approved modes of finance. What is meant here is structuring the PPP programs which can tap financial resources already existing in this region.

The Islamic asset securitisation model

Asset securitisation refers to the process of issuing securities backed by receivables or mortgages and their cash flows. This boils down to sale of debt obligations, which is not permitted under *Shari'a*.

However, the general purpose and obligation of securitisation may not be contrary to *Shari'a*. Hence, we see quite a number of securitisation programs. In an Islamic setting, the securities must represent the ownership of real assets which generate cash flow in the form of rentals or the like.

Therefore, it is possible to pool leased autos and issue securities against the same but then each represents an undivided share in the ownership of the leased cars. The security holder is entitled to get the cash flows generated from rental collection in lieu of their ownership of these autos. The same thing can be done with a pool of leased houses or equipment. Many *Shari'a* boards have applied the rule of majority, thus permitting the inclusion of receivables emanating from auto instalment sales or *murabaha* in the pool, provided the tangible assets remain more than 51 per cent of the pool in terms of value.

While the subject of securities cannot be debt, it can be tangible assets, usufructs or rights but never money.

Securitisation differs from *sukuk* issuance. In the former, investors take the risk of the assets, including the credit risk of the end-users of autos or houses. In the latter, investors take the risk of the issuer entity itself.

Sustainability of *sukuk* issue

'Sustainability' means the capacity to endure. So far, *sukuk* appears to be quite sustainable. *Sukuk* are defined as traded financial instruments representing the undivided beneficial ownership of real assets, rights or usufruct which are characterised by low-risk, limited tenor and predictable income structure. They are not exactly bonds or equity as such. They are a sort of 'hybrid'. It is quite possible for a project to be financed via the issue of *sukuk*. Judging from their rate of growth, *sukuk* have only one way to go: up. On the part of users of funds, they are mega-projects that require significant financial resources on the basis of equity, debt and *sukuk*. *Sukuk* will be quite effective in tapping the huge reservoir of savings, especially in the Gulf region. On the other hand, the growing capital markets in the Gulf region are basically equity exchanges. They are so keen to diversify, and the only way to go is one that is agreeable to the preference of investors and issuers. *Sukuk* will be the best choice.

Recently, some *sukuk* issuers faced difficulties, which brought to the surface the question of whether *sukuk* are sustainable. In fact, almost all of the cases at hand failed due to causes which have nothing to do with the *Shari'a* aspects of *sukuk*. Certainly, *Shari'a* is no guarantee against failure or default. Therefore, we see no reason to doubt the sustainability of *sukuk*.

Refinancing

The standard refinancing program includes replacement of an existing debt obligation with a debt obligation bearing different terms. It is sometimes called 'debt restructuring' or 'rescheduling'. It is resorted to when the indebted entity is having a cash flow problem.

In the language of *Shari'a*, this is a case where creditors are saying to a debtor in distress: 'I will give more time if you give more money (i.e. interest)'. This is the form of usury that no *Shari'a* scholar will dispute the prohibition of. Hence, this refinancing program cannot be applied in the context of Islamic finance.

A small minority of scholars, nevertheless, while firmly upholding such prohibition, permitted joint entry, by the creditor and the indebted entity, into a transaction that creates a new debt, provided that the indebted entity has no difficulty doing the same with a third party. This means he is not sufficiently distressed to the point that others find it too risky to do that. If it were possible to obtain finance from third parties, then it might as well be performed by the creditor himself, even if this were to mean that the new debt would be used to settle the old one.

Credit enhancement in *sukuk* structure

When securities represent simply debt obligation and basically carry credit risk, the credit enhancement will facilitate getting a higher rating by rating agencies, thus attracting more investors and reducing the cost to the issuer.

Schemes like over-collateralisation, reserve accounts, surety bonds and guarantees are standard in this regard.

It is not likely that any these schemes will be used in the context of Islamic finance, simply because *sukuk* are not supposed to be debt instruments; therefore, credit enhancement may not be of much use.

The only thing that resembles a credit enhancement in a *sukuk* program would be the promise to purchase provided by the issuer for the benefit of *sukuk* holders.

In essence, it is an undertaking whereby the issuer, if he fails to make any due payment, promises to buy the underlying assets at par.

Reserve accounts are used in a *sukuk* program but only for smoothing the periodic payments. In some *sukuk* issues, the issuer may extend credit support to the reserve account, meaning that he will be provided liquidity in the form of *Qard Hassan* in case of shortage. But it is always subject to settlement at maturity. No *Shari'a* board has permitted that such a liquidity facility be undertaken by the issuer on its own account.

Islamic finance and non-Muslim countries

Islamic banking is guided and self-regulated by *Shari'a* rules and principles. However, Islamic banking is not itself a religious practice. Therefore, *Shari'a* to Islamic banking is simply a governing law which is not too different in its objective from any other human legal system of justice, equality and fair play. However, it differs in its means and its emphasis on certain aspects of human relationships.

Islamic banking is, therefore, open to everyone. In Malaysia, for example, the majority of Islamic banking customers are non-Muslims, and the Islamic Bank of Britain has many non-Muslim customers. In fact, the first account opened in that bank was by a non-Muslim. Nothing confirms this more than *sukuk*.

One of the earlier issuers of *sukuk* was the state of Saxony-Anhalt in Germany, where *sukuk* were issued by the local government. Corporate *sukuk*, on the other hand, are no longer confined to any geographic boundaries; they are truly global.

We must be very careful in interpreting this fact. Though we think *sukuk* are superior in every respect to conventional bonds, we do recognise that the attracting factor is not this. Since most wealthy Muslim investors will shy away from usury-based financial instruments, to get them to participate in any investment scheme, it must be designed in line with their religious preference.

Notes

1. *Istisna'a* is a *Shari'ah* pre-manufactured procurement contract, the subject of which will be built or manufactured in the future. It is classified in the Islamic jurisprudence as a sale contract.
2. *Ijarah* is a *Shari'ah*-based lease.

7

Islamic Finance and the Regulatory Challenge: The European Case

Ahmed Belouafi and Abderrazak Belabes

Introduction

Islamic finance (IF) came into being no more than five decades ago. Its institutional development can be divided into two phases: that of the 1960s, which witnessed the introduction of a local savings bank in the rural area of Mit-Ghamr in Egypt,[1] and that of the mid-1970s, which saw the introduction of commercial private banking and an inter-government initiative[2] at regional level among OIC[3] countries. Since then, Islamic finance has grown steadily, spreading from one institution in one country to more than 400 institutions in more than 70 countries with total assets reaching the threshold of one trillion US dollars.[4] In addition, its operations have diversified.

As a result, Islamic finance is no longer confined to its traditional home of Muslim and Arab countries; rather, it has spread, in varying degrees, all around the globe. Among the places that have witnessed the emergence of IF is Europe. This chapter addresses issues relating to the regulatory and supervisory challenges in this region by addressing the following questions:

- What are the main regulatory issues that the presence of IF in Europe raises?
- Are a variety of approaches adopted across Europe, or are all the players following the same route?
- Should Islamic financial transactions be taxed on the basis of their legal form or on the basis of their economic substance?

- What are the implications of the authorisation of IF in an EU country for other member states? In other words, does the European passport have an impact on the spread of IF in Europe?
- What are the effects of legal competitiveness in terms of the regulation of IF within Europe?

In considering matters arising from the above questions, the chapter has been divided into six sections. Section I provides an overview of the basic principles of IF, their effect on the structure of a typical Islamic financial institution (IFI) and the policy and tax implications of such an effect. It also gives a brief summary of the latest developments in the IF industry in Europe. Section II then touches upon the nature, rationale and objectives of the regulatory process and their relevance to IF. Section III summarises the variety of approaches adopted worldwide in accommodating IF in conventional systems, and discusses the route pursued by some European countries within the context of these models. Section IV looks at the impact of the European passport on the spread of IF in Europe once a country has authorised the operation of IF domestically. Section V discusses the effects of legal competitiveness on the regulations relating to the presence of IF in European countries. Finally, section VI draws some concluding remarks from the discussion and analysis of the preceding sections.

Section I: Islamic finance – basic principles and its evolution in Europe

I. 1   Basic principles of Islamic finance[5] and their regulatory implications

In order to pave the way for the introduction of IF in any conventional legislative body, it is important to comprehend fully and properly the basic principles that govern the operations of this newly emerging industry. The core foundations of this industry are based upon the rulings of *Shari'a* (Islamic law) that govern matters relating to the ritual as well as transactional dealings of individuals and society. This law provides a general framework within which financial transactions can be conducted. Hence, Islamic finance, in very simple and general terms, can be defined as 'the provision of financial services and products on the principles of Islamic *Shari'a* (law)'.

This definition implies that the main difference between the IF industry and its conventional counterpart centres on the *'Islamicity'* of its operations. So, what are the basic principles that determine this *'Islamicity'*? And what are the legal, regulatory and supervisory implications of these principles?

It is widely accepted that the framework for providing 'Islamic' financial services is guided by the basic principles illustrated in Figure 7.1.

As far as current financial practice is concerned, it is the overarching principle of the prohibition of all forms of interest in financial services[6] (which constitutes the backbone of the operations of conventional finance) and the asset-backing norm that ties the pooling and placement of funds for investment purposes to an underlying tangible or very determined and specified asset or service that have a big impact on the nature of any financial operations being carried out *'Islamically'*. In order to assess the effect of such principles on the operations of a typical Islamic financial institution a theoretical structure for the assets and liabilities of that institution is examined briefly to identify some of the regulatory and supervisory issues that arise from such a structure.

Figure 7.1   Basic principles of Islamic finance

Table 7.1 Theoretical balance sheet structure of a typical Islamic financial institution; policy and/or tax implications of this structure

Assets	Policy and/or tax implications	Liabilities	Policy and/or tax implications
Inventory: Real estate/automobiles.	Distinct characteristic: ownership of assets.	Investment accounts: Deposits assigned for investments are accepted on a PLS basis. That is, neither the principal nor the return is guaranteed. In this category, there are two types of products: general or unlimited, to be used as the IFI sees fit, and special or limited, assigned for particular investments based on customer preference and choice.	Under prevailing laws, deposits and their fixed returns are guaranteed upto certain ceilings through compensation or insurance schemes. How will 'Islamic' deposits be treated, given the fact that return and principal payments depend upon the performance of the financed assets? – Capital adequacy ratios. – Risk management approach. – Corporate governance issues (e.g. moral hazard).

Asset-backed placements: e.g. *murabaha* (cost-plus), *ijarah* (leasing). Finance must be tied to real transactions, be they plant, goods or a service. The IFI must acquire such utilities and bear the associated risks by assuming, at some stage, the ownership of the underlying asset before transferring it to the client. And in providing finance, no pre-determined fixed return (i.e. *ex ante*) can be claimed from the outset of the process. The IFI must share in the profits, if any, and bear part of the losses if that is the case.	No placement of funds in interest-based assets such as bonds and treasury bills. Exclusion of the most widely used instruments for liquidity management, and 'safe' investment opportunities. Double stamp duty or registration tax on assets' double sale. VAT on *murabaha* mark-up. Ownership and illiquidity risks. Rate of return risk. Displacement risk. Equity investment risk.	Current/demand deposits: similar to conventional ones, but no interest or remuneration of any form to be given to customers.	Must be fully guaranteed and subject to customer withdrawal at any time.
Profit-sharing transactions: e.g. *mudaraba* (profit-loss bearing), *musharka* (profit-loss sharing).		Profit equalisation reserves.	Distinct characteristic as prudential tool.

Source: Authors and Islamic Financial Services Board (2010: 17).

It is clear, from Table 7.1, that there are sharp contrasts, at the theoretical level at least, between IFIs and their conventional counterparts. However, at the practical level, convergence between IF instruments and products and their conventional counterparts is dominating the scene through the certification mechanism of scholars and boards (i.e. *Shari'a* supervisory boards (SSBs)), and in some cases lawyers are getting involved in approving the operation of IFIs.[7]

In order to understand the nature of the risks and regulatory concerns associated with IF instruments and operations, three main questions need to be addressed:

First, does the *'Islamicity'* of financial services and products expose institutions offering this type of arrangement to more or less or the same sort of risks that the conventional industry is exposed to?

Second, is it necessary to have an SSB at each and every institution to ensure the *'Islamicity'* of operations?

Third, what are the regulatory implications of such special arrangements?

As for the first question, two views are held:[8] one that suggests minimal regulation if IFIs operate according to the core risk-sharing principles, and one that IFIs must be subjected to the same regulation as their conventional counterparts. There has been a great deal of debate in the literature on this issue. However, the practice in the industry and the attitude of the regulatory authorities in most jurisdictions have been to adopt the latter approach, requesting IFIs to comply with the norms and standards applied to their conventional counterparts. On the other hand, infrastructure bodies of the industry, such as the IFSB,[9] are striving hard to secure the adoption of some modification of the standards developed by international regulators, such as the Basel Committee, to take into account the special features of IFIs.

As for the second question, the development of the industry over the years indicates that ensuring *'Islamicity'* of operations is vital for credibility and public confidence. Practice also reveals that the main way to ensure this is through the appointment of an internal body (SSB) or an individual (scholar) to endorse the *'Islamicity'* of their operations. Wilson[10] noted this fact in relation to the early development of IF in the UK, where some of the conventional institutions offering 'Islamic' products could not attract customers to increase their operations in this area until the appointment of an SSB. Having said that, it must be acknowledged that in recent years *Shari'a* consultancy firms or individuals have emerged as another way of ensuring the *'Islamicity'* of the IF industry. In addition, much debate is taking place about the heavy load[11] that many scholars are taking, which affects the efficiency of their work and may create a conflict of interest between their role as independent advisors and the fact that the managerial committees of IFIs are responsible for their appointment and the remuneration that they get.

As for the third question, several implications are identical to those for IFIs' conventional counterparts. This may be partly due to the dominance of fixed-income products on the assets side of the balance sheets of these institutions through sales and lease contracts. Some of the issues identified by the regulatory bodies are standardisation of products and instruments, information disclosure, corporate governance and capital adequacy requirements. So, almost all prudential matters that justify regulation of the conventional financial industry are relevant to IF as it is practised today.

In this respect, as we will see in a later section, the UK authorities did not see that there was any need or justification for major changes to the existing legislation, as the policy of *'no obstacles, but no special favours'* provided good results by sending positive signals to the industry. It was also considered neither appropriate nor legally possible to vary the UK's standards for a particular type of institution or industry.[12]

I. 2: Evolution of Islamic finance in Europe

The presence of Islamic finance in Europe can be traced back to the beginning of the 1980s in the provision of some commodity *murabaha* on the London market[13] and through the establishment of some financial institutions such as an Islamic insuror (*takaful*) in Luxembourg[14] and Al-Baraka International in London.[15]

Since that time, IF products and institutions have been introduced in various ways in the UK market. However, the dramatic steps in terms of legislation, the establishment of fully-fledged institutions, and the issuance and listing of some Islamic instruments such as the *sukuk* have taken place only over the last few years. At the time of writing, the following facts can be cited as indicators of the development of IF in Europe:[16]

- Europe has five fully-fledged Islamic banks; one is retail, and the rest are wholesale investment banks. All of these institutions are UK-based, but they can increase their outreach in mainland Europe through the European passport, as we will explain in a later section.
- *Sukuk* instruments (or 'Islamic bonds', as some may prefer to call them) are rapidly expanding, too. In the UK since 2006, which saw the first London-listed *sukuk*, transactions in these instruments have exceeded £9 billion through the 26 issues of *sukuk* on the London Stock Exchange.[17] And despite the slowdown in *sukuk* issuance after the financial crisis, 2010 saw the issuance of six *sukuk* in London.[18] In Luxembourg 16 *sukuk* are currently listed on the Luxembourg Stock Exchange (representing approximately €6 billion in notes).[19] In 2004, Saxony-Anhalt became the first state government in Germany (and, for that matter, Europe) to issue a sub-sovereign bond under Islamic principles.[20] And in France in 2008, the AMF (French market regulator) gave permission for *sukuk* to be listed on the regulated financial market.[21]
- Investment funds are also present in some countries of the continent. Luxembourg hosts more than 40 *Shari'a*-compliant investment funds and sub-funds. This constitutes about 7 per cent of all such funds around the world. As a result, Luxembourg is classified among the top five Islamic funds domiciles globally.[22]
- Many European countries have some IF presence in the form of fully-fledged IFIs or through Islamic windows offered by conventional institutions, as Figure 7.2 demonstrates.

Very dramatic growth has been seen in the provision of IF education. According to a recent study, European countries are coming top in terms of the provision of these services, as illustrated in Figure 7.3.[23]

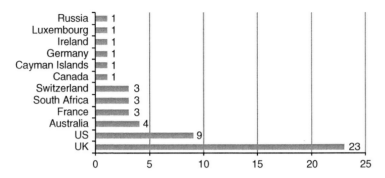

Figure 7.2 Islamic financial institutions and windows in non-Muslim and non-Arab countries

Source: IFSL Research, 2010; Islamic Finance 2010.

It is very obvious, from Figure 7.3, that European countries, especially the UK and France, are playing a leading role in the provision of IF educational programmes at higher institutions. And this position may be consolidated in the coming years, as many other contenders are trying to enter the market.[24]

Section II: Regulatory challenge: nature, objectives and rationale and relevance to IF

It is widely recognised and accepted that financial systems are the most highly regulated activities of the economy. This is mainly due to the fact that financial products and contracts provided by the financial institutions and markets are significantly different from products and services offered by firms in other sectors of the economy.[25] This specialness centres on the role of payment system handling and credit provision and distribution carried out by these establishments. As a result, regulatory authorities in most countries pay particular attention to this issue, in order to maintain the integrity of the financial system, by affecting the behaviour of the regulated institutions and markets[26] in a way that aims at achieving certain objectives. These objectives are considered to be of vital importance to the smooth functioning and stability of the entire economy. Various pieces of legislation and the literature that discusses why financial regulation is beneficial usually state the

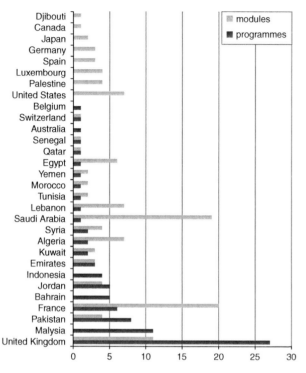

Figure 7.3   Islamic finance programmes and modules provided across the world
Source: Belabes and Belouafi (2011: 17, 24).

following objectives as a mandate that regulatory authorities must aim for:[27]

- Market confidence – maintaining confidence in the financial system of the country;
- Financial stability – contributing to the protection and enhancement of the stability of the financial system;
- Consumer protection – securing the appropriate degree of protection for consumers and users of the financial services and products;
- The reduction of financial crime – reducing the extent to which it is possible for a regulated business to be used for a purpose connected with financial crime.

In addition to the above general objectives for financial activities, these authorities should handle carefully the incorporation of newly emerging industries or products. Therefore, in dealing with the issue of accommodating IF, regulatory authorities try to achieve the following sub-objectives:

- Clarification of the intent of the regulatory authorities to create a level playing field for IF products and institutions. The clarity and intent are a pre-requisite to avoid over- or under-regulation that may either stifle or leave too much room for risk taking respectively.[28]
- A prudential regulation umbrella for Islamic modes of finance as part of the *'no obstacles, no special favours'* policy.
- The same level of regulatory protection for customers of Islamic products and services to boost confidence and stability in the system.

As for the rationale of the regulatory process and its relevance to Islamic financial institutions, the following points can be made:

- Financial innovation often brings with it changes in the perception of risk.[29] Merton makes the point that 'less apparent understanding of the new environment can create a sense of greater risk even if the objective level of risk in the system is unchanged or reduced'.[30]
- Legal: Do existing laws in secular jurisdicitons allow financial transactions to be governed by *Shari'a* principles?[31] Practice reveals that there is no problem here, as existing laws are flexible enough to accommodate innovations and new products as long as they are well understood and they do not bring excessive risks that are beyond control. Although this is the case, we must admit that there is cultural and historical sensitivity[32] to the issue of IF operations in Europe, especially if emphasis is given to the inclusion of certain religious laws within the mainstream secular ones.
- Regulatory: Do Islamic financial institutions and products require similar levels of supervision to conventional ones?[33] We discussed this point in detail in the previous section, and we concluded that most regulatory authorities, especially the European ones, are of the opinion that IFIs must be subject to the same existing prudential regulations as their conventional

counterparts whenever that is possible, without subjecting the institutions of this newly emerging industry to stringent constraints that will penalise their customers or affect the innovation process that is so vital because the industry is still in its infancy. So, the main point is to strike a balance between over- and under-regulation, either of which may send the wrong signals to interested players, parties and markets.

Section III: The European approach within the context of the various approaches adopted[34]

Cross-country practices and examination of regulatory and supervisory authorities in various countries reveal that there are four main approaches, as summarised in Figure 7.4, adopted in accommodating IF in conventional systems. The fifth approach in the figure, that is the approach of Kuwait, falls under the auspices of the third, i.e. the dual, but it is shown separately to highlight its specialness in two respects: the first is that the established institution, although it is a depository one, has been given the name of a house rather than a bank, and the second is that it is regulated by the Ministry of Commerce rather than the Central Bank of Kuwait.[35]

Apart from the case of Kuwait, the figure is self-explanatory in dividing conventional systems accommodating IF into four categories according to the level of change: the first represents the status quo; the second involves minimum changes to existing laws; the third is the creation of special laws for the regulation of IF activities that go hand in hand with conventional laws; and the fourth,

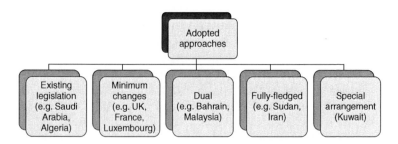

Figure 7.4 Approaches adopted worldwide in accommodating Islamic finance

which is very limited, is the conversion of the full system to an Islamic one. It is clear that, so far, the European approach falls within the second category, minimum changes to existing laws. In what follows, we will look at the experiments of three players in this context: the UK, France and Luxembourg, and then we will provide a brief account of the latest development in other countries, such as Italy and Germany.

III. 1.   The experiment in the UK

The United Kingdom is, by far, the most active player in the area of accommodating IF in its territory. Many conventional institutions operating on the London market have been active in the provision of *Shari'a*-compliant products since at least the beginning of the 1980s. However, much of the significant development has taken place over the last few years.[36] Among these evolutions are the legislative measures taken by the government to provide a level playing field for the IF industry. In 1995, the then-governor of the Bank of England, Sir Edward George, recognised the 'growing importance of Islamic banking in the Muslim world and its emergence on the international stage' as well as the need to put Islamic banking in the context of London's tradition of 'competitive innovation'.[37]

After that recognition, no significant step was taken by the British government until 2001, when a high-level working group, chaired by Baron George, was established to identify the barriers that IF faces in the UK.[38] According to George, the analysis undertaken by the working group followed the steps outlined in Figure 7.5.[39]

From the time of the formation of the working group, the British government took several initiatives before attaining the current level of development and growth of IF in the UK. Among the measures

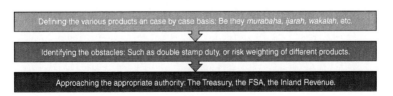

Figure 7.5 Steps followed by the working group chaired by Sir Edward George

taken was the formation of more specialised groups such as the Tax Technical Working Group (TTWG), which looks at tax issues, and the circulation of various consultation papers in order to get a wider perspective from stakeholders in the industry: the Treasury, the FSA, the Inland Revenue, the Muslim community, *Shari'a* experts, the IF industry and its infrastructure institutions such as the IFSB and AAOIFI, the City, lawyers and consultancy firms. In addition, the process was guided by clear principles[40] and objectives.[41] This lengthy work has resulted in the identification of several obstacles. Among them are:

- The definition of a deposit and how to reconcile legal requirements under the English law with the IF principle of the prohibition on the taking and giving of interest without linking it to the performance of an underlying asset.
- The double stamp duty land tax (SDLT) on the purchase of the property by the bank from the seller and the re-sale of that property to the customer (the purchaser) through the various modes of IF available for home purchase, such as *murabaha, ijarah* or diminishing *musharaka*.[42]
- The role of the *Shari'a* advisory board, and if it is going to interfere and overlap with that of the managerial committee, the shareholders and the general assembly of the institution.
- Transparency, clarity, information disclosure and the promotion of products and services.
- Standardisation of products and accounting information.

In overcoming the above hurdles and other issues, the practical steps taken by the various groups and official entities involved in the overall process of providing a level playing field for IF are depicted in Figure 7.6.[43]

Figure 7.6 Practical steps derived from the UK experiment in regulating Islamic financial activities

It can be seen from the above account that the process has been lengthy and thorough in order to avoid unintended or undesired outcomes. Moreover, the tax treatment of IF instruments has been guided by a process based on the economic substance of these instruments rather than the legal form. In the official document published by the government at the end of 2008, those principles were spelled out as follows:[44]

1. Treatment should follow the economic substance of the transaction;
2. Treatment should be on the same basis as equivalent financial products that bear interest;
3. Ordinary tax rules should be applied where possible; and
4. Rules that give undesirable or unpredictable results should be amended.

The UK authorities started the process of introducing legislation in the Finance Act of 2003, which removed the double SDLT on an *'Islamic mortgage'* through the *murabaha* and *ijarah* modes of finance. And in subsequent years, more legislation was introduced, which is summarised in Table 7.2.

In granting the licence to the Islamic Bank of Britain (IBB) in 2004, the UK authorities in collaboration with the IBB authorities came to the following solution with regard to the issue of 'deposit': 'legally depositors are entitled to full repayment to fulfill the FSA requirements, however, customers have the right to turn down deposit protection and choose instead to be repaid under the *Shari'a*-compliant risk sharing and profit bearing formula'.[45] And with regard to the issue of *Shari'a* compliance, the policy adopted was that there will be no central *Shari'a* board at the FSA or the Bank of England, as applied in other jurisdictions like Malaysia. This is because the FSA is a secular regulatory entity, and interfering in this area may limit financial innovation in this newly emerging and promising industry.[46] So, in the end, it was left to individual institutions to choose the appropriate method of ensuring the *'Islamicity'* of their operations. However, the FSA stresses that the information given in this respect must not be misleading.

Table 7.2   Examples of changes introduced between 2003 and 2010

Date	Introduced Changes
2003	Removal of the double charge of stamp duty land tax (SDLT) for *murabaha* and *ijarah* contracts that allow individuals to purchase homes. Other measures were introduced to offer Islamic products for child trust funds, asset finance and ISAs.
2005	Extension of the removal of double SDLT to diminishing *musharaka* (another mode of alternative finance) and the introduction of deposit arrangements.
2006	Extension of removal of double SDLT to beneficiaries (i.e. companies) and the introduction of *wakalah* (profit-share agency).
2007	Discussion of applying the same tax rules for conventional debt instruments like bonds to *sukuk* (Islamic bonds or alternative finance investment bonds).
2008	Dealing with more issues relating to the issuance of *sukuk*.
2009	Legislative measures for SDLT, capital gains tax (CGT) and capital allowance rules for land transactions involved in the structuring of *sukuk* instruments.
2010	The Financial Services and Markets Act 2000 Order 2010 exempts alternative finance investment bonds, a class of debt-like security which includes *sukuk*, from collective investment scheme (CIS) regulations.

Sources: www.hm-treasury.gov.uk; www.fsa.gov.uk; www.londonstockexchange.com

Despite the positive steps and initiatives taken by the British regulatory authorities, there are deep issues that are of much concern to IF customers in the UK, including:

- Are *Shari'a*-compliant products and services really 'Islamic' given the fact that more emphasis has been given to compliance with conventional legislation than to compliance with Islamic finance principles?[47] In this respect, one might mention the way the issue of deposits has been treated. Does the customer's choice have any legal weight if a customer chooses the 'Islamic' way when a dispute arises between him or her and the bank?
- How to make sure that the information given to a customer is not misleading? Is it enough to have just the signature or stamp of the

'extensively' used scholars to ensure '*Islamicity*'?[48] Or to provide general and brief information about the products, and when it comes to the signing of the deal, very lengthy and complicated contacts?

The above issues are just some examples of the concerns raised by customers, most of whom are still reluctant to use these products. We are aware that some of the issues raised (especially the latter ones) may apply to conventional products as well, but there is a big difference between the two cases. Conventional practices and contracts are well established and understood, and the laws that regulate disputes are clear, and legal expertise is widely available. On the other hand, it must also be stressed that what the British government has done with respect to IF, many Muslim and Arab countries have failed to do, so the points raised must be read within this context and within the framework of scientific enquiry, which requires a balanced and rigorous examination that puts every opinion, policy and analysis in perspective.

III. 2.   The experiment in France

Despite the fact that France is home to the largest Muslim minority among the EU countries, and the fact that French banks have played an important role since the mid-1980s in offering *Shari'a*-compliant products in the Gulf region and elsewhere, France only recently became active in the area of IF. At the end of 2008, French authorities took a proactive attitude in promoting Paris as a European hub for IF. France's goals in this respect are twofold: attracting global funds to French soil, and making France more competitive in the area of IF.[49] The authorities have looked into how legislative amendments can be made to attain these goals. The process went through various stages, and at the end the authorities concluded: 'IF should not need any exceptional consideration under French law; the only point is that the structure of the products should be examined on a case-by-case basis, institutions and customers using Islamic financing schemes should receive the same level of protection as under conventional schemes, and any issues that arise should be dealt with in the existing framework'.[50]

Table 7.3 gives a summary of the most important developments that have taken place since 2009.

Table 7.3   Measures taken by the French authorities to accommodate Islamic financial products and operations

Date	Event
February 3, 2009	The Islamic Finance Committee of Paris Europlace stated in its 2009 work programme the need to adapt the French trust system to allow the issuance of *sukuk* in French law.
February 25, 2009	French tax-planning framework for *sukuk* and *murabaha*.
March 18, 2009	Senator Philippe Marini proposed an amendment to the civil law and the trust system (Régime de fiducie) to develop the French financial system and facilitate the issuance of *sukuk*. The Senate adopted the law.
September 9, 2009	Member of Parliament Chantal Brunel proposed a disposition in favour of IF as part of a bill facilitating SME financing.
September 17, 2009	The Parliament adopted the bill after heated debate.
September 18, 2009	60 parliamentarians of the opposition filed a censure motion to the Constitutional Council.
October 14, 2009	The Constitutional Council censured Article 16 concerning Islamic Finance.
August 24, 2010	Publication of tax instructions on *sukuk, murabaha, ijarah* and *istisna'a*.

After the failure of the French government to pass laws for IF through the Parliament, it seems that the French approach has turned to the route of tax instructions for accommodating various IF products. As noted by Thierry Dissaux, Islamic financial advisor to the Minister for the Economy: 'We were led to see things differently because, on reflection, we felt that there may be no need to adjust the legal framework. If a bill is required, we will present it; but if it appears that we have a scheme as efficient, or more so, without legislative adjustment, I do not see why the question would arise'.[51] This approach is guided, like the British one, by the economic substance of the contract rather than the legal structure and 'analysis is likely to privilege the economic and financial reality over the legal form of transactions. The operations will be analysed and supervised not by assumption of their legal components, but, as far as possible, by examining their final economic effect'.[52]

III. 3. The experiment in Luxembourg

As mentioned in section I, Luxembourg has engaged in IF since the beginning of the 1980s, but its legislative initiative took off only in 2008. In April 2008, the Ministry of Finance formed a task force to identify obstacles to the development of IF and to pave the way for its growth.[53] In 2009, the government asked the tax authorities to examine the characteristics of IF products and to come up with solutions that would provide a level playing field with respect to their conventional counterparts. In early 2010, the Ministry of Finance produced a comprehensive document[54] detailing the regulatory and tax treatment of IF transactions and operations in Luxembourg. In that document, more emphasis was given to investment funds, private equity, venture capital, real estate investments and wealth management. However, the document also discussed tax treatment relating to well-known modes of finance such as *murabaha* and *sukuk* as a continuation of an early circular issued by the tax authority in this regard.[55] The main guiding principle in these procedures was to treat the revenues of IF products as if they 'were interest'.[56] Once again, it will be noticed that this approach is akin to that of the UK.[57]

III. 4. The experiment in Spain

Spain's interest in Islamic finance goes back at least to the end of the last century.[58] The Spanish Islamic Assembly recommended, after the seminar 'Alliance of Civilizations, Alliance for Peace' held on 18th and 19th June 2007 in Cordoba, the promotion of *halal* and ethical banking and financial products for a more humane economy and a better redistribution of wealth.[59] According to Silvia Cerrada, secretary of the Association for the Promotion of the Rights of Muslims, *Shari'a*-compliant financial products would be extremely popular in Spain, especially for the acquisition of real estate.[60] La Caixa and Banco Santander, two leaders in their sectors of activities (respectively, the first bank and the first savings bank in Spain), launched current accounts and interest-free financing for the Muslims of Spain. The banking entity Bancorreos (the Spanish postal service), in cooperation with Deutsche Bank and in accordance with the Halal Institute (Instituto Halal), plans to offer its customers an Islamic service.[61]

At the regulatory level, Spain will undoubtedly draw on the experience of the civil law country that is leading this area (France), avoiding the requirement that the introduction of Islamic finance should be legislated. The path to introduction is therefore limited to changes in taxation intended to erase the disparities that penalise the instruments of Islamic finance as compared to conventional instruments. Hence, tax instructions will facilitate the development of Islamic finance through *'no obstacles, but no special favours'* by making the Islamic instruments as competitive as their conventional rivals and keeping them as the exclusive preserve of credit institutions or the stock exchanges.

III. 5.   The experiments in other EU countries

In other European countries, not much work has been done except awareness programmes in the form of seminars or conversations organised by some regulatory authorities, such as the Banca d'Italia,[62] Italy's central bank, to give authorities the opportunity to understand the reality of IF and its regulatory and supervisory implications for the host countries. To date, there are varying views with regard to the presence of IF in these markets. One of these views, held by the Italian regulators,[63] is to let market forces decide when IF may enter their country; the other is rather sceptical and doubtful about the presence of IF in European countries. This latter view is held by BaFin, the German financial regulator. From the various sources consulted, it seems that the German financial sector is less open to IF products despite a few specific initiatives, such as the issuance of *sukuk* by Saxony-Anhalt, a federal state of Germany, in 2004. One the most important obstacles mentioned to explain this attitude is the difficulty of bringing IF products up to German standards of reporting and supervision.[64] That may explain, to a certain degree, why some big German banks, such as Deutsche Bank, prefer to offer IF products in London rather than Frankfurt.

Section IV: IF and the European passport

It is well known that under an EU directive, in order to qualify for licensing, financial products and services must meet basic requirements or 'threshold conditions'[65] that are set out to protect consumers and investors alike.[66] Once these requirements are met in a member state, a licence is then granted by the 'home state regulator' to the applying firm. That firm is thereby enabled to carry out business in these regulated activities in other EC Member States (the 'host states') under the so-called principle of mutual recognition of authorisation and of prudential supervision systems: the European passport.[67]

The passport is meant to allow Islamic or conventional banks to provide their products throughout the EC Member States. Thus, a bank like the British Gatehouse Bank[68] can offer its Islamic financial products in France. Gatehouse Bank has taken this opportunity to become the first Islamic bank to join the Paris Europlace, an organisation that promotes Paris as a financial centre. Richard Thomas, CEO of Gatehouse Bank, says about this first step that it demonstrates a commitment to export its Islamic finance experience from London to Paris: 'We have an ambitious French project underway which is ongoing and looking at France as a jurisdiction for Islamic finance to internationalise the reach of Islamic finance as a mode of finance'. This project may be extended 'to any mature economy in Europe that is interested to learn from the experience in London', he added.[69]

The European passport can be exercised:[70]

- by way of free establishment, i.e. by establishing a branch or subsidiary to engage in retail or corporate banking; or
- by way of providing financial services.

Note that under European Commission regulations the European passport is limited to the licensed activities granted in the home state, but these are mutually recognised by the host Member State in which the products are provided. So, in principle, it is possible that the passport would give its holder the opportunity to expand its operations in host countries. However, as far as the operations of IF are concerned, there are some issues that might present obstacles to benefiting from the passport gateway. One of these is the non-uniform definition of a 'bank' or 'credit institution', as established by the European Commission directive. For instance, the German, the French and the UK jurisdictions seem to take a broader perspective on terms of reference than is provided for by the European definition.[71] The other issue is the absence of a unified regulatory framework with regard to accounting, reporting and information disclosure in the EU to monitor Islamic finance activities. In this context, BaFin, the financial regulator in Germany, has raised some reservations, as mentioned before, about the qualification of an Islamic bank for a banking licence at the European level; among them was the issue of the accounting, reporting and auditing techniques developed and adopted in Europe.[72]

Section V: Effects of legal competitiveness on the regulation of IF

Legal competitiveness means that the law has become a competitive factor to be taken into account at two levels: corporate and state. At the corporate level, it is necessary to strengthen the role of law in key decisions that corporations have to take, and at the state level, a particular country must enhance the legal attractiveness of its domestic financial market by providing to investors a competitive legal environment, not only for offering financial services and products but also for settling disputes in cases of conflict. The former French Justice Minister Michèle Alliot-Marie mentioned this fact at a UNESCO conference held in 2010 in relation to the French position on this matter: 'It is now a policy of the financial centre to strengthen the financial competitiveness of Paris. I want a policy from the financial centre to strengthen the legal competitiveness of Paris'.[73]

At the extraordinary general meeting of the national bar association held on October 15, 2010, in Paris, the Economy Minister of France, Christine Lagarde, announced that she had asked Michel Prada, former president of the Financial Market Authority, to form a think tank to look at the legal competitiveness of the French financial system.

Within the context of legal competitiveness, it is important to distinguish between two perceptions; the first treats the competition between legal systems as a war or zero-sum game,[74] and the second looks at it as 'an attempt to copy what is done elsewhere'.[75] As far as IF is concerned, it seems that the two postures are present in the practices of countries entering this domain. On the hand, we find that every country is trying, through the welcoming of IF, to enhance the attractiveness of its financial centre, but on the other hand, rivals coming late to the race seem to copy what their predecessors have done. For the latter argument, we have seen the influence of the UK experiment on others, and for the former it seems that, in dispute settlements in IF matters, every country in this very competitive world tries its utmost to gain an edge over its rivals. In the case of IF, it seems that dispute settlement will be of vital importance. France has carried out an extensive study to review the feasibility of letting the French courts and judicial system play a significant role in this area.[76] Malaysia, on one hand, is trying to position its laws as 'the law of choice for Islamic finance transactions globally', and Dubai, on the other hand, through the International Reconciliation and Arbitration Centre, is aiming at establishing a very specialised body that deals with disputes relating to IF. Both jurisdictions see themselves as more appropriate since 'the underlying laws don't provide a sufficient platform to satisfactorily resolve disputes'.[77] However, the UK is working hard to consolidate its position as it is already a very well-established and recognised jurisdiction in these matters. Its officials have said on many occasions that IF is there to stay and prosper. For other European countries, there is not much debate, but if Spain develops the strategy of welcoming IF within its borders, it may play a gateway role for Latin American countries. The main conclusion that can be drawn from this point is that countries that have not yet entered the IF race may look to the strong points they have, especially in the areas of law and regulation on the one hand, and education on the other. However, there are deep issues that need to be taken into consideration in this respect. One of these issues has been spelled out by Merton, who stated that 'applying uniform rules to different financial institutions and functions, to countries at different stages of economic development and with different cultures, can create inefficiencies and/or unfair competitive disadvantages, with negative consequences for collective welfare.[78] The other is a difference of opinion on *Shari'a* matters among the various jurisdictions, especially between the Gulf and the Malaysian ones Malaysia. These differences are likely to affect the emergence of a unified dispute body that will be globally acceptable to industry players, lawyers and legislative entities in the near future.

Section VI: Concluding Remarks

The above analysis and discussion with regard to the issue of accommodating IF in European conventional systems reveals that there is a spectrum of views, ranging from the more receptive and welcoming to the sceptical and doubtful. The UK is an example of the former; Germany the latter. In between the two opposing views, some other countries are adopting a 'wait and see' policy to let market forces impact the direction of the swing. Furthermore, the European experiments show that the main work has concentrated on tax treatment, looking at the economic substance of IF transactions rather than the legal structure of the contracts, to provide a level playing field for this newly emerging industry, and to avoid, as much as possible, engaging in the legal process, which is cumbersome. It might be very difficult and time-consuming to pass laws through the legislative bodies. The French have tried that route, but they could not overcome the very sophisticated and sensitive hurdles that arose. Matters arising from the regulation of IF in Europe are highly affected by the approach taken by the UK authorities. However, mainland civil law countries, such as Spain and Italy, are now looking to the French experiment, which represents a typical reference for a civil law country. Overall, there are good lessons and important practical steps to be learnt from the European approaches to regulating the activities of Islamic finance in conventional systems, especially the well-established financial centres.

Finally, despite the current trend, the legal framework of Islamic finance in European countries is likely to change within the global context of legal competitiveness, where each country seeks not only to improve the intelligibility, predictability and clarity of its law, but also to adapt legal measures to the new markets.

Notes

1. The experiment is well known for its founder, Ahmed El-Naggar, and it lasted for four years, from 1963 to 1967.
2. The Islamic Development Bank (IsDB), which has been transformed into a group with many subsidiaries and affiliates.
3. Organization of the Islamic Conference.
4. *Al-Iqtisadia* newspaper, 'Experts: Saudi Arabia Is Capable of Becoming a Pillar in Islamic Finance in the World', No. 6372, 23 March 2011. The paper also reported that some experts predict that, by the year 2020, *Shari'a*-compliant assets would be around USD 4 trillion.
5. It is important to note that some of these principles, such as the prohibition of *riba* (or usury) and speculation are shared by other

religions, cultures and national laws. As noted by Alain Couret, Professor of Law at the University of Paris 1–Panthéon-Sorbonne, at the Saudi-French 'Dialogue of Civilizations' symposium on 15 March 2010: 'There was no gap between Islamic finance and French law, although it is secular, because it is essentially Christian and bears the traces of prohibitions common to monotheist religions, among them usury and speculation. The law also is in favour of the idea of sharing; France is a country of mutual insurance'; quoted by Habib Trabelsi, 'Finance islamique: un mariage de raison … presqu'au point mort, *Saudiwave*, 19 April 2010.

6. Financial Services Authority, 2006, 'Islamic Banking in the UK'.
7. El-Gamal, 2006, *Islamic Finance: Law, Economics and Practice*, p. xi.
8. El-Hawary et al., 2004, 'Regulating Islamic Financial Institutions: The Nature of the Regulated', p. 28.
9. The Islamic Financial Services Board, a Malaysia-based body that was created by a group of central banks in 2002 with IMF and BIS support as an international standard-setting organisation that promotes and enhances the soundness and stability of the Islamic financial services industry by issuing global prudential standards and guiding principles for the industry. www.ifsb.org, accessed 27 February 2011.
10. Wilson, 1999, 'Challenges and Opportunities for Islamic Banking and Finance in the West: The United Kingdom Experience', p. 438.
11. Funds@Work research reveals that the top two scholars are on more than 70 boards. Funds@Work, 2010, 'The Small World of Islamic Finance', p. 7.
12. Ainley et al., 2007, 'Islamic Finance in the UK: Regulation and Challenges', p. 11.
13. Wilson, 2007, 'Islamic Finance in Europe', p. 2.
14. Krawczykowski and Ammar, 2010, 'Clear Commitment: Luxembourg Tax Authorities Issue Guidance on Islamic Finance'.
15. Wilson, 1999, 'Challenges and Opportunities for Islamic Banking and Finance in the West: The United Kingdom Experience', p. 426.
16. IFSL Research, 2010, 'Islamic Finance 2010', p. 3.
17. Walmesley, 2011, 'Another Year of Growth and Development for the London Stock Exchange Markets for Islamic Finance', p. 2.
18. Ibid.
19. Krawczykowski and Ammar, 2010, 'Clear Commitment: Luxembourg Tax Authorities Issue Guidance on Islamic Finance'.
20. The Banker, 2004, 'Global News: Germany Launches Europe's First Sukuk'.
21. Autorité des Marchés Financiers (AMF), 2008, 'Admission to Listing of Islamic Bonds (Sukuk) on a French Regulated Market'.
22. Luxembourg for Finance, 2010, 'Luxembourg Vehicles for Islamic Finance Structures', p. 7.
23. Belabes and Belouafi, 2011, 'Features and Trends of Islamic Finance Programs at Educational Higher Institutions across the World'.

24. The last two years has seen significant development in the UK and Spain in this area through the establishment of specialised Islamic economics and finance centres at Aston Business School in 2010 and at IE-Business School in Madrid in 2009. Moreover, the Russian Finance University, which is considered to be among the top five universities in Russia, is showing interest in IF. One member of staff at this university who paid a visit to our centre (the IERC) on 20 February 2011 indicated their intentions regarding this.

25. Llewellyn, 1999, 'The Economic Rationale for Financial Regulation', p. 5.

26. Ibid., p. 6.

27. These objectives have been drawn from the statutory objectives given to the Financial Services Authority in the UK (www.fsa.gov.uk). The Banking Act 2009 stressed the same objectives for the regulation of banking institutions: Objective 1 is to protect and enhance the stability of the financial systems of the United Kingdom; Objective 2 is to protect and enhance public confidence in the stability of the banking systems of the United Kingdom; Objective 3 is to protect depositors; Objective 4 is to protect public funds (HM Treasury, 2009, Banking Act 2009). Moreover, some other important central banks, such as the European one, have concentrated on one of these objectives, for example, 'the overriding objective of [the ECB] monetary policy is price stability'.

28. El-Hawary et al., 2004, 'Regulating Islamic Financial Institutions: The Nature of the Regulated', p. 28.

29. Ibid., p. 3.

30. Merton, 1995, 'Financial Innovations and the Management and Regulation of Financial Institutions', p. 462.

31. Hesse et al., 2008, 'Trends and Challenges in Islamic Finance', p. 179.

32. Wilson, 2007, 'Islamic Banking – Opportunity or Threat?'

33. Hesse et al., 2008, 'Trends and Challenges in Islamic Finance', p. 179.

34. For an in-depth analysis of the variety of models adopted and their progressive nature see Belabes, 'Variety of Legislative Models in Welcoming Islamic Finance', forthcoming article in *Les Cahiers de la Finance Islamique*.

35. El-Hawary et al., 2004, 'Regulating Islamic Financial Institutions: The Nature of the Regulated', p. 27.

36. For more details about the latest developments of IF in this country see Belouafi, 2011, 'Islamic Finance in the UK: The Regulatory Challenge'.

37. Ainley et al., 2007, 'Islamic Finance in the UK: Regulation and Challenges', p. 8.

38. Ibid.

39. George, 2003, 'Towards Islamic House Financing in the UK', p. 77.

40. These are fairness, collaboration and commitment. HM Treasury, 2008, 'The Development of Islamic Finance in the UK: The Government's Perspective', pp. 13–14.

41. These are enhancing the UK's competitiveness in financial services by establishing the UK as a gateway for international Islamic finance, and ensuring that everybody, irrespective of their religious beliefs, has access to competitively priced financial products. HM Treasury, 2008, 'The Development of Islamic Finance in the UK: The Government's Perspective', p. 13.

42. In this process the bank pays the price in full on the spot and adds to it a margin (mark-up), and the customer pays the due amount in deferred instalments during the agreed-upon period. So, it is clear that there is a double sale that requires a double charge of SDLT if tax changes have not taken place.

43. For a typical example of these steps through the legislation of *sukuk*, see Belouafi, 2011, 'Islamic Finance in the UK: The Regulatory Challenge'.

44. HM Treasury, 2008, 'The Development of Islamic Finance in the UK: The Government's Perspective', p. 15.

45. Ainley et al., 2007, 'Islamic Finance in the UK: Regulation and Challenges', p. 14.

46. Ibid., p. 13.

47. In this respect one can understand the argument of the FSA, as a secular regulator that has nothing to do with the certification of religious verdicts, but regulators, as noted by Wilson, should make sure that proper procedures are in place for ensuring *Shari'a* compliance; Wilson, 2003, 'Regulatory Challenges Posed by Islamic Capital Market Products and Services', p. 1. We think this matter could be dealt with within the general framework of corporate governance that the regulators require of the firms that are granted licences to carry out financial services transactions.

48. This issue 'raises concerns over the ability of Sharī'ah scholar boards to provide enough rigorous challenge and oversight of firms' products and services'. Christophe, 2010, 'The French Licensing Authority Faced with Globalization of Islamic Finance', p. 171.

49. Christophe, 2010, 'The French Licensing Authority Faced with Globalization of Islamic Finance', p. 168.

50. Ibid., p. 173.

51. Dissaux, 2009, 'Finance islamique: 2010, l'année de la réussite?'

52. Christophe, 2010, 'The French Licensing Authority Faced with Globalization of Islamic Finance', p. 171.

53. Luxembourg for Finance, 2010, 'Luxembourg Vehicles for Islamic Finance Structures', p. 1.

54. Ibid.

55. Administration des Contributions Directes, Circulaire L.G.-A, pp. 3–5.

56. Ibid.

57. HM Treasury, 2008, 'The Development of Islamic Finance in the UK: The Government's Perspective', p. 16.

58. Lorca and Orozco, 1999, *La banca islámica sin intereses: Elementos básicos*.

59. Contreras, 2007, 'Hacia la creación del primer banco islámico en España'.
60. Molina, 2008, 'La banca española ensaya ofertas que cumplan con el islam'.
61. Alonso and Coispel, 2009, 'Finance islamique: quelle possibilité de développement en Espagne?', p. 73.
62. In November 2009, the Bank of Italy organised an awareness seminar on Islamic finance, discussing its relevance to Europe in general and to Italy in particular. Official delegates from the central banks of Italy and Malaysia, as well as academics from the UK and Italy, attended the seminar. For more information see www.bancaditalia.it.
63. Donato and Freni, 2010, 'Islamic Banking and Prudential Supervision in Italy', p. 197.
64. Engles, 2010, 'German Banking Supervision and Its Relationship to Islamic Banks', pp. 179–180; Jouini and Pastré, 2008, *Enjeux et opportunities du développement de la finance islamique pour la Place de Paris*, pp. 97–98.
65. Briault, 2002, 'Revisiting the Rationale for a Single National Financial Services Regulator', p. 2.
66. Foot, 2003, 'The Future of Islamic Banking in Europe'.
67. Khan and Porzio (eds), 2010, *Islamic Banking and Finance in the European Union: A Challenge*, p. 3.
68. A wholesale investment bank that was granted a licence by the FSA, the UK single regulator, in 2006.
69. Parker, 2009, 'UK Islamic Bank Gets Foothold in France'.
70. The Commission of the European Communities, 2004, 'European Passport Rights for Credit Institutions Regulators', p. 2.
71. Khan and Porzio, 'Islamic Banking and Finance in the European Union: A Challenge', p. 4.
72. Engles, 'German Banking Supervision and Its Relationship to Islamic Banks', p. 180.
73. Alliot-Marie, 2010, 'Discours d'ouverture des conférences du droit et de l'économie'.
74. du Marais, 2008, 'L'attractivité économique du droit français et le rôle des professions juridiques', p. 2.
75. Baïssus, 2010, *Compétitivité juridique*.
76. Affaki et al., 2009, 'Rapport du Groupe de travail sur le droit applicable et le règlement des différends dans les financements islamiques'.
77. *Business Week*, 2010, 'Malaysia Challenging U.K. as Hub for Sukuk Law: Islamic Finance'.
78. Montanaro, 2010, 'Islamic Banking: A Challenge for the Basel Capital Accord', p. 113.

References

Administration des contributions directes, 2010, Circulaire L.G.-A n°55 du 12 Janvier, Luxembourg.

Affaki G., Fadlallah I., Hascher D., Pézard A., Train F-X., 2009, 'Rapport du Groupe de travail sur le droit applicable et le règlement des différends dans les financements islamiques', 21 September.

Ainley M., Mashayekhi, A., Hicks, R., Rahman, A., and Ravalia, A., 2007, 'Islamic Finance in the UK: Regulation and Challenges', Financial Services Authority.

Alliot-Marie M., 2010, 'Discours d'ouverture des conférences du droit et de l'économie', UNESCO, Paris, 25 June. Available at: www.presse. justice.gouv.fr/archives-discours-10093/les-discours-de-2010-11742/ ouverture-des-conferences-du-droit-et-de-lecono mie-unesco-19853.html.

Alonso, J. I., and Coispel, A., 2009, 'Finance islamique: quelle possibilité de développement en Espagne?', *Revue Banque Stratégie*, February, No.170, p. 73.

Arnaud A., 2010, 'The French Licensing Authority Faced with Globalization of Islamic Finance', in Khan M. F. and Porzio M. (eds) *Islamic Banking and Finance in the European Union: A Challenge*, Cheltenham–Northampton: Edward Elgar, pp. 167–174.

Autorité des Marchés Financiers (AMF), 2008, 'Admission to Listing of Islamic Bonds (Sukuk) on a French Regulated Market', 2 July. Available at: www.paris-europlace.net, accessed 27 February 2011.

The Banker, 2004, 'Global News: Germany Launches Europe's First *Sukuk*', 1 September. Available at: http://goliath.ecnext.com, accessed 27 February.

Baïssus J.-M., 2010, *Compétitivité juridique*, Paris: Fondation pour le droit continental, Lettre d'information novembre.

Belabes A., 2011, 'Variety of Legislative Models in Welcoming Islamic Finance', forthcoming article in *Les Cahiers de la Finance Islamique*, No. 3, Strasbourg Business School, University of Strasbourg.

Belabes, A. and Belouafi, A., 2011, 'Features and Trends of Islamic Finance Programs at Educational Higher Institutions Across the World', Paper presented at the 10th Meeting of the Heads of Economics and Islamic Economics Departments at Saudi Universities, IERC, Jeddah, 15 March.

Belouafi A., 2011, 'Islamic Finance in the UK: The Regulatory Challenge', forthcoming article in *Les Cahiers de la Finance Islamique*, No. 3, Strasbourg Business School, University of Strasbourg.

Briault C., 2002, 'Revisiting the Rationale for a Single National Financial Services Regulator', Occasional Paper Series 16, Financial Services Authority, February.

Business Week, 2010, 'Malaysia Challenging U.K. as Hub for *Sukuk* Law: Islamic Finance', www.businessweek.com, 7 September.

The Commission of the European Communities, 2004, 'European Passport Rights for Credit Institutions Regulators'. Available at: www.mjha.gov.mt/DownloadDocument.aspx?app=lom&itemid=10426.

Contreras, J., 2007, 'Hacia la creación del primer banco islámico en España', *el Economista*, 22 June.

Dissaux, T., 2009, 'Finance islamique: 2010, l'année de la réussite?', Interviewed by Hanan Ben Rhouma, Saphirnews.com, 23 December.

Donato L. and Freni M. A., 2010, 'Islamic Banking and Prudential Supervision in Italy', in Khan M. F. and Porzio M. (eds) *Islamic Banking and Finance in the European Union: A Challenge*, Cheltenham–Northampton: Edward Elgar, pp. 189–206.

El-Gamal, M. A., 2006, *Islamic Finance: Law, Economics and Practice*, Cambridge: Cambridge University Press.

El-Hawary, D., Garis, W., and Iqbal, Z., 2004, 'Regulating Islamic Financial Institutions: The Nature of the Regulated', World Bank Policy Research Working Paper, 3227, March.

Engles J., 2010, 'German Banking Supervision and Its Relationship to Islamic Banks', in Khan M. F. and Porzio M. (eds) *Islamic Banking and Finance in the European Union: A Challenge*, Cheltenham–Northampton: Edward Elgar, pp. 179–180.

Financial Services Authority, 2006, 'Islamic Banking in the UK', Briefing Note BN016/06, 9 March. Available at: www.fsa.gov.uk.

Foot M., 2003, 'The Future of Islamic Banking in Europe', Speech delivered at the Second International Islamic Finance Conference, Dubai, 22 September.

Funds@Work, 2010, 'The Small World of Islamic Finance', Funds@Work & Zawya Shariah Scholars, Version 5.0, 5 October.

George, E., 2003, 'Towards Islamic House Financing in the UK', *Review of Islamic Economics*, No. 13, pp. 73–78.

Hesse, H., Jobst, A. A., & Solé, J., 2008, 'Trends and Challenges in Islamic Finance', *World Economics*, April–June, Vol. 9, No. 2, pp. 175–193.

HM Treasury, 2008, 'The Development of Islamic Finance in the UK: The Government's Perspective', The Treasury, London, December.

HM Treasury, 2009, 'Banking Act 2009', The Treasury, London, February.

IFSL Research, 2010, 'Islamic Finance 2010', IFSL in collaboration of UK Trade & Investment and City of London, January.

Islamic Financial Services Board, 2010, 'Islamic Finance and Global Financial Stability', report published by IFSB in collaboration with IsDB & IRTI, Kuala Lumpur, April.

Jouini I. and Pastré O., 2008, *Enjeux et opportunités du développement de la finance islamique pour la Place de Paris*, Paris: Paris Europlace.

Khan M. F., and Porzio M., (eds), 2010, *Islamic Banking and Finance in the European Union: A Challenge*, Cheltenham–Northampton: Edward Elgar, UK.

Krawczykowski, R., and Ammar, A., 2010, 'Clear Commitment: Luxembourg Tax Authorities Issue Guidance on Islamic Finance'. Available at: www.islamica-me.com, accessed 7 March.

Llewellyn David, 1999, 'The Economic Rationale for Financial Regulation', The Financial Services Authority, UK.

Lorca, A., and Orozco, O., 1999, *La banca islámica sin intereses: Elementos básicos*, Madrid: Agencia Española de Cooperación Internacional.

Luxembourg for Finance, 2010, 'Luxembourg Vehicles for Islamic Finance Structures', Luxembourg for Finance, Luxembourg, April.

Marais B., du, 2008, 'L'attractivité économique du droit français et le rôle des professions juridiques', Université Paris 10, 1 October. Available at: www.u-paris10.fr/.../com.univ.collaboratif.utils.LectureFichiergw?

Merton R., C., 1995, 'Financial Innovations and the Management and Regulation of Financial Institutions', *Journal of Banking and Finance*, No. 19, pp. 461–481.

Molina, M., 2008, 'La banca española ensaya ofertas que cumplan con el islam', 18 February. Available at: www.webislam.com.

Montanaro E., 2010, 'Islamic Banking: A Challenge for the Basel Capital Accord', in M. F. Khan and M. Porzio (eds) *Islamic Banking and Finance in the European Union: A Challenge*, Cheltenham–Northampton: Edward Elgar, pp. 112–127.

Parker M., 2009, 'UK Islamic Bank Gets Foothold in France', *Arab News*, 9 October.

Walmesley, G., 2011, 'Another Year of Growth and Development for the London Stock Exchange Markets for Islamic Finance', *London Stock Exchange Islamic Finance Review*, November, p. 2. Available at: www.londonstockexchange.com.

Wilson R., 1999, 'Challenges and Opportunities for Islamic Banking and Finance in the West: The United Kingdom Experience', *Thunderbird International Business Review*, Vol. 41, No. 4/5, pp. 421–44.

Wilson R., 2003, 'Regulatory Challenges Posed Islamic Capital Market Products and Services', IOSCO Task Force on Islamic Capital Market.

Wilson R., 2007a, 'Islamic Banking – Opportunity or Threat?' *Common Ground News Service (CGNews)*, 23 January. Available at: www.commongroundnews.org.

Wilson R., 2007b, 'Islamic Finance in Europe', Robert Schuman Centre for Advanced Studies, European University Institute, RSCAS PP 2007/02, Florence, Italy, December.

Web sites:

- en.wikipedia.org
- goliath.ecnext.com
- www.bancaditalia.it
- www.commongroundnews.org
- www.fsa.gov.uk
- www.hm-treasury.gov.uk
- www.ifsb.org
- www.islamica-me.com
- www.londonstockexchange.com

8
Islamic and Ethical Finance: Taking Responsibility in a Post-crisis Context?

Olivia Orozco de la Torre

Since Umer Chapra, an expert on Islamic finance and a former advisor to the Saudi Arabia Monetary Authority, published his classic work *Towards a Just Monetary System* in 1985, several international financial crises have followed.[1] After the Asian financial crisis of 1997, as well as the one that began ten years later in the United States and has been responsible for the current economic crisis, different voices and debates have arisen, calling for the revision and redefinition of the global financial system, to bring it closer to the real economy and to curtail speculation.

In Islamic finance, those returns derived from financial speculation are considered illegitimate, because, on the one hand, they entail an excessive, arbitrary risk (*gharar*), like hazard games, while, on the other, they do not result from any real effort or work. Revenues are justified only if they result from labour or from certain involvement in a real risk, related to a real economic activity, be it production, manufacturing, trade or services. Therefore, Islamic financial institutions act as commercial intermediaries or investing institutions, but they neither invest in nor deal with conventional financial institutions nor speculate with financial derivatives in conventional capital markets.

By keeping themselves away from high-risk financial products and speculation, as well as by screening out companies with high levels of debt, Islamic financial institutions have managed to be less affected by the subprime crisis, and the subsequent 2008 financial crisis, than other financial institutions.

Not being ruled by interest rates, and thus being free from their fluctuations, their returns are associated with the performance of real projects and activities. It is therefore claimed that this is a much fairer, more stable and more responsible alternative for allocating resources than the current financial system, which is governed by fraud and disequilibrium.

Islamic economists, devoted to building the theoretical economic model in which Islamic finance is framed, consider the conventional financial system unfair because it implies a net transfer of resources from those with scarcity to those with abundance. As a result, they consider that it contributes to increasing, rather than decreasing, social disparities, undermining the justice and equilibrium principles that should characterise society in an Islamic worldview.

In the aftermath of the crisis, Islamic finance thus joins forces with other voices around the world in calling for a more moral and responsible way of doing finance, such as ethical investment funds or ethical banking. Lots of commonalities can be identified between them. Both ethical and Islamic finance bring values to the front by giving them a key role in allocating resources. Moreover, most of these pivotal values, such as justice, solidarity and responsibility to the common good or the community's welfare, are shared by both types of financial intermediation. In that way, both systems look for socially responsible ventures and investments, caring for sustainability and social justice while excluding from their portfolios and investments types of activities and firms that, in many cases, also collude (e.g. arms manufacture and trafficking, alcohol, pornography and gambling). In addition to barring participation in pork-related industry, Islamic finance is distinct in that it prohibits dealing with interest-based products and institutions, as well as in holding a stronger position against speculation and in promoting real-economy-oriented projects and investments. Although that is the case for some segments within ethical and community-based finance, Islamic finance is intended to play, in principle, a much more active role in promoting growth, employment and development. In that sense, it brings together the negative discriminating criteria of ethical finance and the positive, proactive nature expected of socially responsible enterprises and microfinance.

Having said this, the international economic crisis has shown that, indeed, Islamic financial institutions have not necessarily been playing that developmental role. In fact, if Islamic finance has not been totally isolated from the impact of the crisis, it is partly due to the particular concentration of its activity on real estate investments, especially in the Gulf. In addition to import and export financing, real estate markets have basically centred their activities on the issuance of *sukuk* or Islamic certificates for financing big urban developments. As a result, Islamic finance, and in particular the *sukuk* industry, was very much affected by the end of the property bubble in some Gulf countries, by the resulting fall in prices and by Dubai's financial crisis (an impact that is reflected in the parallel performance of real estate prices and *sukuk* emissions in the region from 2004 to 2009, see Figures 8.1 and 8.2). Some of DP World's debt that had to be postponed and renegotiated in December 2009 was in the form of *sukuk*, issued that same year by Nakheel, one of the companies of the group. These difficulties debilitated and brought the whole industry to a standstill, if only temporarily.

In 2010, calmed by Abu Dhabi's rescue and Dubai's debt restructuring, and stimulated by the economic recovery in the region, the *sukuk* industry recovered, with a total of USD$51.2 billion being issued in this type of certificate, beating 2007's record figures. Moreover, during the first quarter of 2011, a total of USD$32.4 billion was issued, according to the last report by the *Financial Times*.[2]

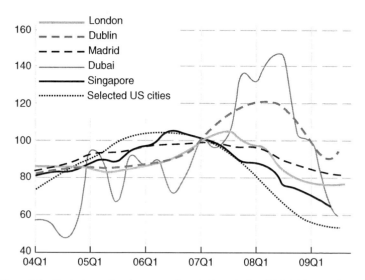

Figure 8.1   Evolution of real estate prices (urban; index 2007, Q1 = 100)
Source: Regional Economic Outlook: Middle East and Central Asia, IMF, 25/05/10

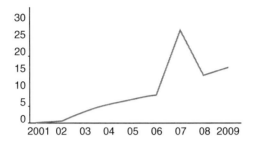

Figure 8.2   World *sukuk* issuance (USD billion)
Source: *Islamic Finance: Global Financial Stability*, IDB, IRTI, IFSB, April 2010

Even if the bad patch is over, it is important to take note of some of the problems that it revealed. First of all, although Islamic finance was safe from financial speculation in international markets, this is not the case in the real estate sector. This may distort the economy and not always lead toward an equilibrated and sustainable growth path. Second, while development-focused in its conception, and origins (e.g. Mit Gahmr, Tabung Hajji, IDB), in the past few decades, for different reasons it has favoured the expansion of commercial banks over development banks, concentrating on financing trade and real estate acquisitions, and on being based on mark-up financial instruments instead of profit-and-loss-sharing contracts, those better portraying the fair and cooperative ideal of Islamic finance.

Even if, as most Islamic finance practitioners argue, the link to the real economy is still there, much more can be done to contribute to the development of their societies. Not charging interest and revenues, depending on the performance of those projects financed, it was expected that Islamic finance institutions would better allocate resources towards those more viable and efficient projects, which in turn will have a higher impact on employment and growth. Being community-conscious and socially responsible, they were also projected to make positive discriminations towards those projects that could better contribute to the development of the whole community. Moreover, its Islamic character was thought to facilitate reaching whole sectors of the population, especially in rural areas, outside the conventional financial system, and thus to contribute to a process of credit formation and endogenous development in those areas, in a similar way to microcredit instruments.

All of these aspects have not received sufficient attention, thus raising demands and self-criticism from within the industry and opening the debate about the need to prioritise values over principles; intention over form. Those points emerged during the round-table at Casa Árabe that closed the seminar 'Beyond the Crisis: Islamic Finance in the New Financial Order', which was organised with the IE Business School and King Abdulaziz University at Madrid, in June 2010, and which discussed the growth and potential of alternative finance in the aftermath of the crisis. As Professor Asutay argued then, in Islamic finance institutions and instruments, 'form' but also 'substance', is expected to be Islamic.[3] In this vein, some Islamic scholars and practitioners are calling for turning from mere *Shari'a*-compliant towards *Shari'a*-based or -rooted products.

The development of the *sukuk* industry has broadened the possibilities for investing through Islamic finance tools. Indeed, *sukuk* are being used to fund a variety of projects with important developmental impact, from infrastructure and transport to water and manufacturing, which may contribute to a more inclusive form of growth. However, much more needs to be done in this direction if Islamic finance really wants to become a vehicle for transforming, improving and developing the society where it operates.

Islamic finance has been demonstrated to be viable and compatible with modern economies. It is now accepted globally to be an efficient and productive way of financial intermediation. Moreover, as Professor Asutay defended, it has even surpassed the category of a mere niche market.

However, in the post-crisis context, Islamic finance, like ethical finance, should make a further step towards being defined, not so much by what it rejects (by the negative criteria used to scrutinise investments), but by what may be its active contribution to social and economic development,[4] that is, by doing a bit more and taking responsibility for social welfare.

Notes

1. More than 100 since 1945, as pointed out by that same author in another article, quoting C. Reinhart and K. Rogoff, 2008, 'Banking Crises: An

Equal Opportunity Menace', NBER Working Paper No. 14587, in M. Umer Chapra, 'The Global Financial Crisis: Can Islamic Finance Help?', *New Horizon: Global Perspective on Islamic Banking & Insurance*, No. 170, January–March 2009, pp. 20–3.

2. 'Good Omens amid Turbulence' *Islamic Finance Financial Times Special Report*, 12 May 2011.

3. Mehmet Asutay, 'Islamic Finance: Ethicality and International Developments and Trends', 'Beyond the Crisis: Islamic Finance and the New Financial Order', Center for Islamic Economics and Finance (IE), Center for Islamic Economics (KAAU), and Casa Árabe, 16–17 June 2010.

4. 'We need to look not just at what we can't invest in – we need to look at what we should invest in', Naveen Raza, Cru Investment Management, as quoted in 'Islamic and Ethical Finance: On the Same Path?', *New Horizon: Global Perspective on Islamic Banking & Insurance*, No. 170, January–March 2009, pp. 10–12.

Index

Page ranges given in bold indicate the entire chapter, or discussion topic, for which the entry is the main subject.